the little brown church in the vale...

...when did the lights go out?

GERALD,

THANK YOU FOR DISAGREE-
ING WITH ME. IT IS
ALL OVER THIS WORK AND
THAT IS WHAT MAKES
IT WORK.

THANKS

[signature]

DISCLAIMER: The thoughts and opinions contained in this work are entirely those of the authors and are not directly endorsed by the Tusculum Cumberland Presbyterian Church, its staff, leadership, or members of the congregation, unless otherwise noted. This book is not endorsed by the Cumberland Presbyterian Denomination, any of its boards, agencies, or publications.

the little brown church in the vale...

...when did the lights go out?

A look at the dying twenty-first century denominational movement and maybe its only hope

Bob G. Shupe

With contributing authors:
Terrie Gray, Billy Hensley, Ronnie Pittenger,
Gerald Tomerlin, Karen Williams and John Wilson

The Little Brown Church in the Vale…When Did the Lights Go Out?
A Look at the Dying Twenty-first Century Denominational Movement and Maybe Its Only Hope

Copyright © 2008 Bob G. Shupe. All rights reserved. No part of this book may be reproduced or retransmitted in any form or by any means without the written permission of the publisher.

Published by Wheatmark®
610 East Delano Street, Suite 104
Tucson, Arizona 85705 U.S.A.
www.wheatmark.com

International Standard Book Number: 978-1-60494-137-1
Library of Congress Control Number: 2008929188

"Church is the only society on earth that exists for the benefit of its non-members"

> William Temple
> Archbishop of Canterbury
> 1881–1944

Contents

Foreword ix
Preface xi
A Special Thanks xv
Introduction xvii

Chapter 1:   So What Is Small? 1
Chapter 2:   So How Do Churches Remain Small? 12
Chapter 3:   Why Did The Lights Go Out? 23
Chapter 4:   Denominational or Nondenominational 37
Chapter 5:   Organized Boxes 43
Chapter 6:   Why Do Churches Fail? 47
Chapter 7:   The Sequoia Lesson 65
Chapter 8:   Our Journey: The Tusculum Story 72
Chapter 9:   Our Journey: Relating to the Body 78
Chapter 10:   Our Journey: The Body of Christ in Action 87
Chapter 11:   The Pastor 107
Chapter 12:   In Conclusion of Things 114

Notes 119
About the Author 121
Contact Information 123

Foreword

I consider it an honor to be invited to write a word for my dear Christian friend, Bob Shupe, and his latest book. It has been my privilege to work alongside Bob for the past thirty-plus years. He was reared in a Christian family and has been part of the Christian church all of his life. Therefore, he has a deep rooted love for God and the works of God. He has a strong sense of God's calling in his life, as you will discover while reading this book.

I have found, over the years, that Bob epitomizes the old saying of a person who talks the talk and walks the walk. He is a doer and not a hearer only. He is an active Christian, loves his Lord, works hard in the church, and believes that the Bible is the Word of God and that, outside of a personal faith in Jesus Christ, there is no hope for anybody to get to heaven. He is a leader among God's children. He has great compassion for the lost in the world. As you read this book, you will note that he is very observant and understands what is happening in the Christian church during this generation.

While you are reading this book, take time to think about what is being said. You will sense Bob's great love for the church. You will also discover thoughts you have never considered before. Our church family has grown to understand that Bob thinks outside the box. I've always seen Bob as one who has one foot in the box and the other outside the box while maintaining a deep love for the church and a compassionate concern for the world. This book will certainly cause you to think about what's going on at the beginning of the twenty-first century in the church and in the world community. More than that, it will give you a glimpse of how God is working in our world and how we as individuals and as a church can better serve and reach this generation for Him.

Ronnie Pittenger, Pastor
The Tusculum Cumberland
Presbyterian Church
Nashville, Tennessee

Preface

A Faithful Tradition of Practicing What You Preach

As you read this book, you will be challenged to take a fresh look at the direction in which your ministry and that of your church points. Does it point inward toward existing ministries and maintaining status quo or outward, extending to your community and the world? My first inclination was to give all of the profits from this book to our church. Then it occurred to me that I hadn't learned much from my own writing. My daughter attended college with a special young lady by the name of Jara Sturdivant, who has dedicated her life to Word Made Flesh. This organization requires that those who work with them raise their own salaries through fundraising and sponsors. My wife and I have been honored to be one of Jara's sponsors for some time. The profits from this book will go to Jara and her life's work with Word Made Flesh. She is a very worthy servant and it is an honor to support her and this ministry. Practicing what we preach, none of the profits from this book will go to our church. Thanks to God for showing us how important it is to stop looking inward and cast off the anchor of maintenance that often holds us in place instead of moving forward in our corporate and individual ministries.

A Word about Word Made Flesh

History

Word Made Flesh was started in 1991 as a nonprofit 501(c)(3) organization that exists to serve the poorest of the poor around the world. In 1994, Word Made Flesh initiated its first children's home in Madras, South India, for abandoned babies, with a primary focus on pediatric AIDS care. In 1995, another home was established for severely mentally and physically disabled girls who have been abandoned, left on the streets to die.

Since then, Word Made Flesh has expanded into other countries in South Asia, South America, and Africa, where they serve with international Christians to make Jesus, the living Word, flesh among the poorest of the poor. Their current projects include pediatric AIDS care, rehabilitation for abused and destitute women, care and education for the war-affected, residential care for children with mental and physical disabilities, advocacy for street children, housing and rehabilitation for children and youth of the streets, and protection and prevention for sexually exploited women and children.

Preamble

"We are a fellowship of believers united in obedience to the Lord Jesus Christ for service among the poorest of the world's poor. We submit to Kingdom spirituality, which faces the harsh realities of a broken world and seeks to respond as Jesus would... and indeed will. This submission increasingly facilitates the life and redemptive ministry of Jesus in purity and power at work within us, extending to the lost and dying. We yield to the Holy Spirit who alone exalts Jesus drawing all to Himself, that through us, Jesus may be free to give Himself away."

Mission Statement

We are called by Jesus Christ to birth communities which practice the presence and proclamation of the Kingdom of God among the poorest of the poor. These Kingdom communities will be placed and nurtured within the two-thirds world mega-cities. We believe nationals have the greatest opportunity for the intense identification necessary for on-going transformation among the urban poor.

Our method is incarnational. Our means is community.

Our involvement includes advocacy for the poor, ministries of compassion and proclamation of the Good News. We exist that Jesus, the Living Word, be made flesh.

Vision Statement

Word Made Flesh is called and committed to serving Jesus among the poorest of the poor. This calling is realized as a prophetic ministry for, and a holistic, incarnational ministry among, the world's poor. We focus our energy to make Jesus known among the poor while reconciling the Church with the poor.

Our involvement for the poor is primarily through serving the Church as a prophetic voice articulating God's passion for the poor through Scripture and further educating them concerning the needs of the world. We seek to reconcile the Church with the poor as a means of communicating and testifying of God's redemptive work in our lives. This movement of bringing the Church and the poor together is done through Biblical preaching, teaching, discipleship, exposure experiences, music, media, and other creative means. As we participate in this movement we pray that our lives will answer both the cry of God for the poor and the cry of the poor for God.

Partnership Information

Our ministry among the poor is through partnership with national believers. Our focus is the most vulnerable among the poor: women and children. We seek to assist local churches and believers in the initiation of development, relief and care projects that have on-going transformational potential. This is done through partnering with and through local churches and national believers. Through partnership as a worshipping and serving community, we grow mutually in our understanding of holistic incarnational ministry. We pray that any Word Made Flesh presence will stand as an abiding illustration of the Kingdom of God. Go to www.wordmadeflesh.org for further information.

A Word about Jara

Jara spent her early years in Indiana and Michigan but claims Franklin, Tennessee, a city just south of Nashville, as home. It was in Franklin that she accepted Christ at her local church. From elementary school to high school, Jara learned about Christ's love for others through mission trips, her family, and church. At Asbury College, she learned more about Christ's love for the poor, but she didn't know in what capacity she could serve Him. Jara graduated from Asbury in 2003 with a bachelor of arts in journalism and went to Memphis to work toward her master's in journalism at the University of Memphis.

In Memphis, Jara put the puzzle pieces of her life together. Through the university she worked with *The Teen Appeal*, a citywide high school newspaper for Memphis City Schools, and had an aha moment. She realized that everyone needs the chance to know and show their potential and that no one should be looked down upon because of age, race, or affiliation. Jara received her master's degree in journalism in August. God brought Jara to WMF through Stephanie McGuire, former assistant to the director. Now, as the advocacy coordinator, Jara continues to seek God's heart for the poor.[1]

A Special Thanks

The concept for this book was born through my relationship with some very special people. These individuals are coauthors of this book and deserve a lot of the credit not only for their contributions, but for their inspiration and encouragement to finish this work. My heartfelt gratitude goes to:

> Terrie Gray
> Billy Hensley
> Ronnie Pittenger
> Gerald Tomerlin
> Karen Williams
> John Wilson

In addition to those mentioned above, I would like to thank Tim Baranoski for his indepth thoughts and analysis of this work. Tim is currently a ministerial student at Memphis Theological Seminary studying to become one of the pastors who will have an opportunity to make a difference. He will.

And there is something more than inspiration, something that comes from someone who has dedicated her life to you and you to her, my bride. Thanks to Valerie, my bride for thirty-nine years. Thanks for allowing me to sit and express myself on a laptop during what little free time we have together. However, we have learned that God continues to multiply what time is left over. He has done that with not only our time but our love, our family relationships, and our finances. Simply put, I am so blessed!

Most of all I thank my Lord for giving His life so that I might have such blessed opportunities.

Introduction

Like many folks in America, I grew up in a very small church. The church was built next to a bluff, just off the main road running between Norton and Wise in southwestern Virginia. Located across the main highway sat the two-room schoolhouse where I completed first and second grade. The school and the church both relied on outdoor restroom facilities. The community, Esserville, had everything it needed. There was a post office not much larger than an outhouse, a feed store, a gas station where someone came out and pumped gas for you and cleaned your windshield, and a small dry-goods store. Most folks grew their own vegetables and wrung the neck of a chicken in the backyard for Sunday dinner (lunch for those in certain parts of the country). Many in the community attended church somewhere on Sunday Morning.

Most of these churches, like my childhood church, still exist today. Many of them have remained the same size even though the communities have grown around them. Some of these churches are now located in the middle of very populated areas, swallowed by urban expansion. Yet there has been no growth within these churches. The little brown church in the vale, as represented in the song, "The Church in the Wildwood" by Dr. William S. Pitts, has become just the *little* church down the street.

Considering the scripture Mark 16:15 "Go into the world. Go

everywhere and announce the message of God's good news to one and all," how did it happen that these churches remain small? More important, why has it happened over and over again to thousands of churches of all denominations across our country? When you consider the plan of salvation, how can a church *not* grow? In a perfect world, the New Testament church growth in the book of Acts should be experienced in every church and body of believers. You would remind me, only in a *perfect* world.

This is not a simple problem. However, some would contend it is not a problem at all. Some go so far as to defend a no-growth philosophy and create seminars to develop ministries for small churches as if it is their ministry to remain small. I believe there are several reasons that churches do not grow. Some of these are not reasons, but mindsets. Other no-growth excuses include lingering myths about people not being able to know everyone in a large church, entertainment replacing ministry, and commercialization of the gospel.

Perhaps the real issues might include loss of control and simply not having a circle-of-life experience in place for those who are brought into the church. A circle of life as it relates to the church is a circle starting with new members' conversions and continuing until they reach a point of maturity, at which time they introduce others to Jesus. This is not a perfect circle. In fact, it may not even resemble a circle. The point is that every Christian should eventually take someone to heaven with them. That is Christ's command, not my musing. The fact remains that if a church, any church, is fulfilling the Great Commission and introducing others to Christ, there will be growth—end of sentence, period, no discussion. So why are churches not growing? Worse, why are we satisfied with the situation?

There is one other issue at the heart of this debate, an issue that is sensitive and in some cases combative. It is the issue of the twelve-letter bad word, *denomination*. Some denominational churches see the results of the nondenominational church movement and falsely believe that the answer lies in ignoring their own heritage and ability to connect to other "like" churches (connectionalism). They think if only they could shed the negative connotation of their denomination and its exclusively conferred status and become a community church, then the chains would drop off and there would be instant growth. From my experience their success or failure may not lie in their name, but in reliance on someone else (the denomination) to do their ministering, outreach, teaching, and development. A few will come to a church because it has a denomination name on its sign; most will not. People are attracted to a church because people, who are the church, invite them to come to a church that has intentionally developed unique ministries for their community. You might want to de-emphasize the denominational connection, but it would be a mistake to abandon it. If you don't agree with what your denomination is doing, fix your own local church problems first, and then God can use you to help the larger community. One of the primary requirements of leadership is that the leader's house is in order. This takes a lot of sacrifice and simple hard work. If your own local church is not in order, you have zero credibility in trying to direct the recovery of another failing church or denomination.

These issues, connectivity, attitude, intentional circle-of-life teaching, and others, are what I want to address in this book. However, a totally different subject involves churches that have grown and then for many different reasons, declined. Most of these churches never come back to where they once were. If you are involved in either one of these congregations, small or declining, I pray that you will not reject these ideas. I also don't expect you to embrace all of them. I hope that you will at least evaluate your church's mission and satisfy yourself that your church's lack of growth is not justified. Please take this journey with me.

Postscript

The song referred to earlier, "The Church in the Wildwood" by Dr. William S. Pitts, has an interesting correlation to the intent of this book. Dr. Pitts, born in Orleans County, New York, in 1830, discovered a perfect spot for a church just after moving to Bradford, Iowa, from Wisconsin in 1857. By 1864, during the Civil War, the church was finally dedicated, though unfinished inside. Dr. Pitts fell in love with the church and its beautiful spot in the vale. Before the church was built, Dr. Pitts wrote the words to this song but never shared them with anyone until the dedication service. The song was soon published and became a standard for many church worship services.

The theme of the song is straightforward. It speaks of the beautiful church and its surroundings. It filled the mind of a man who remembered the church from his childhood. It speaks of the sweet tones of the ringing bells. The third verse changes abruptly to memories of someone the writer has lost who is buried on the site. The fourth verse ends by saying that the writer will join that individual at the writer's death. All of the verses are followed by a chorus that chants, "Come, come, come to the church by the wildwood."

The song raises a question relative to the reason some attend a certain church for years and never see any growth. Other than the fact that the church sits on a beautiful spot and someone the writer loves is buried there, is there any other reason I would want to become a part of this church? In the end it seems that the little church had the same problem many churches have today. Until I read this story, I had never really thought about the term "brown" in the song. Why was the church painted brown? I always thought of the church being pure white and sitting in the middle of a golden field of waving wheat. As many times as I have sung this song, it had never occurred to me that the church was brown. According to the story it was "for want of money to buy better paint, some say." Well, so much for evangelism and stewardship in Bradford, Iowa, in 1864. Are we enchanted with the church structure, or are we passionate about telling others about Jesus Christ?

I found the following on the actual website (www.littlebrownchurch.org) of this church recently:

History took another turn when the Weatherwax Quartet

traveled throughout Canada and the United States in the 1920s and '30s. Their theme song was "The Church in the Wildwood" and they talked about the little church. After World War I, highways were improved and cars brought many visitors. When a school superintendent and a merchants' daughter were married at the church, a new tradition was started. Over 40,000 visitors come to the Little Brown Church each year, and over 400 weddings are performed annually. In June of 2005, wedding number 72,000 was held at the church. The congregation is alive and well with an active Sunday School, youth groups, choirs, ladies' fellowship, Bible study, a prayer chain group, and weekly services at 10:30 on Sunday. They remain, as they were founded, a Congregational church. The song continues to be sung in a little church that is painted brown and sits in the wildwood.[2]

The more things change, the more they stay the same.

One

So What Is Small?

Many terms are relative. Small belongs in that category. In an effort to define church size, a new word has been enlisted: mega-church. While that term certainly brings to mind Willow Creek, Saddleback, and others, it does little to draw distinct lines between large churches and the majority of churches in America. These mega-churches have, unintentionally, redefined how most people view church. In most people's minds, small is anything that does not reach the standards of these very large congregations.

These large churches are to be commended and praised for the work they are doing. I praise the Lord every time I pass one of them or hear of the work they are doing for the Lord and His kingdom. Not to be overlooked, however, is that with every additional opportunity created by a large church, there come additional problems, failures, and responsibilities. It is my opinion that God is not impressed by the size of these churches. Unfortunately, in some cases they become a place for Christians to hide, to become just a number and not become involved in completing the circle of Christian growth. It is also my opinion that God is equally unimpressed by a small church. In all cases God looks at the heart of the individual. He cannot do that if His criterion involves size. The purpose of this discussion is not to find fault with mega-church ministry, but rather to take a look at the opportunities available to the *rest* of God's kingdom and the reasons those opportunities are not being explored or, in some cases, intentionally ignored.

First, which small is good and which big is bad? What determines the size of a church? Is it determined by the number of people who attend? Not really; it is determined by the number of people who are *not* there, and I'm not talking about those who stopped coming because they got their feelings hurt. I'm talking about the thousands of unchurched, probably unsaved people in a rural community and the hundreds of thousands in urban settings.

Is small always better than big or vise versa? No, in fact that is the wrong question. Size is not relative to effectiveness of ministry. However, the end result of ministry is directly related to the effectiveness of ministry. It is wrong for a small church to sit still and die because they cannot find a pastor. He is not your answer. Rather, each member, in any size church, has an obligation to minister and introduce others to Christ. In an article dated March 19, 2007, a survey released by the Barna Group indicates that the unchurched population in America is approaching one-hundred million.[3] How many of those do you need to double the size of your church? Can you have a big church (by most denominational standards approximately three hundred members) in a rural setting? Probably not, but you can double the size of your church. The current members of your church will know many of these unchurched folks. If you, the lay people, will grow spiritually and commit to the principles of individual evangelism, example ministry, and the principle of community evangelism (simply inviting people you know to church), growth will never be a problem, and you will not stop at doubling your congregation and, consequently, the citizens of Heaven.

Okay, big church member, you are feeling mighty good about now. You say to yourself, "this book is not about me or my church." Wrong. Why did *you* stop growing? You answer, "Well, we hit that two hundred or three hundred mark and it seemed like we hit a wall." Well, probably not. You just got too busy and forgot your purpose. Administration took the place of evangelism. Introducing others to Christ dropped from the number one spot. No program or facility in the world will draw people and perpetually retain them without constant effort. There are empty health clubs all over this country that prove that doesn't work. Even big churches stop growing. If evangelism, discipleship, and missions (foreign and domestic) are not first, second, and third on your list of priorities, find a good real estate agent or increase your dues and put a country club sign out on the street to comply with truth in advertising ethics.

Here is the bottom line: every church is small! The army has a bumper sticker, "An army of one." You are the church and you are a congregation of one; it doesn't get much smaller. Grow your own church and invite others to celebrate and praise the Lord with you at your meeting place, the church building. Then let the size of the building be determined by the number of Christians who are doing what Christ commanded in Mark 16:15: "Go into the world. Go everywhere and announce the Message of God's good news to one and all." This passage is from, the *Message*, by Eugene Peterson, published by NavPress Publishing Group and first copyrighted in 1993. It is a modern day translation, which will be used throughout this book, unless otherwise noted.

Let's dig a little more beneath the surface.

So what really is small? Large can be defined as thousands, but what about a church of nine hundred? Is that small? What about four hundred? One hundred fifty? Thirty? My definition of small is probably a bit outside the box. I believe *any* church is small that is not actively, intentionally focusing on God's call to ministry. A church that is not actively, intentionally focusing on God's call to ministry is always going to be smaller than it could be and therefore small. A church should be compared to itself, not to its neighbor. This thought may be outside the box, but it is as inside the box as it gets when considering John 15.

John 15:5–8 says, "I am the Vine, you are the branches. When you're joined with me and I with you, the relation is intimate and organic, the harvest is sure to be abundant. Separated, you can't produce a thing. Anyone who separates from me is deadwood, gathered up and thrown on the bonfire. But if you make yourselves at home with me and my words are at home in you, you can be sure that whatever you ask will be listened to and acted upon. This is how my Father shows who he is—when you produce grapes, when you mature as my disciples."

Jesus does not suggest that individuals and therefore churches should be compared to each other but to themselves as they relate to Him. There are two things that are suggested here that affect growth and decline. First, in respect to a church declining, if the body of the church is pulling away from Him and its true purpose, the church begins to die and thus shrinks. This reduction has nothing to do with the intervening hand of God. On the other hand, it could be that the church, and therefore the individuals within the church, is being pruned away by God. If this is the case, then the church will eventually begin to grow. Second, only through much prayer and discernment of God's will can the church and the individuals that make up the church decide what is happening. Some may try to fool themselves and others, but all will know what is really happening. Some may just be too stubborn to admit it. Sadly, some may not be spiritually mature enough to know the difference.

Larger churches are most likely doing, and have been doing for some time, the things necessary to follow God's call. That is why they are large. However, these churches also have their challenges.

Growth should never stop. A church is either growing or dying. There is no middle ground. Consider the writer's words to the church in Laodicea, recorded in Revelations 3:15–17, "I know you inside and out, and find little to my liking. You're not cold, you're not hot—far better to be either cold or hot! You're stale. You're stagnant. You make me want to vomit. You brag, 'I'm rich, I've got it made, I need nothing from anyone,' oblivious that in fact you're a pitiful, blind beggar, threadbare and homeless." The Laodician Church was stricken with apathy for God's truth. They were self-centered. Laodicea, now modern Pamukkale (Western Turkey), was the wealthiest city in ancient Phrygia. They had it all. The church had become captivated by its own culture. Later in that same chapter we read the familiar words in verses 20 and 21, "Look at me. I stand at the door. I knock. If you hear me call and open the door, I'll come right in and sit down to supper with you. Conquerors will sit alongside me at the head table, just as I, having conquered, took the place of honor at the side of my Father. That's my gift to the conquerors!" There are three things that can happen in response to this verse. You may not be able to hear the knock; you might ignore the knock, or you can answer the door. Two of these three things produce terrible consequences.

Maybe the Laodician church was so busy with other things that they did not hear him knock. Or worse, they heard the knock but did not answer the door. We can assume from this scripture that if we do not answer his knock, He will not come in, and He will not eat with us. Laodicea began the process. They were a church, but they were not doing what God wanted them to do. He knew their deeds. They were not on fire for His kingdom. In short, they were not *growing* in Him. Whatever was initiated at the founding of the Laodician church had come to a halt. They were dying.

The third thing we can do is answer the door. That is most likely the choice that has been avoided by many small churches across this country. Maybe the church has treated God's knock like it was an unwanted salesman. Maybe some churches have not answered the door because they are so spiritually feeble.

An interesting point was raised recently during a small group Bible study regarding our answering the door when Jesus knocks. It was suggested that perhaps the reason many in our churches never grow spiritually past a casual relationship with Christ is that all they do is answer the door. Perhaps it is assumed that if a person answers the door that Jesus will be invited to eat with the host and develop a relationship. Is it possible that Jesus is invited in and then simply stands in the corner waiting to be invited to the table? It is certain that Jesus will not force himself on us so it would follow that it is our responsibility to accept all of His invitation. When you gaze across your congregation, and know the public involvement of each member, is it possible that your shortage of leadership is because people choose to eat alone?

Whatever the reason, it is difficult for any church to justify dismissing God's call to ministry, the result of which is a dying congregation. Refusing to follow God's call to ministry defines any size churches inability to grow. Attrition is increasing at an alarming rate in a number of churches, some to the point of extinction.

The American Society for Church Growth reported the following in 1999 to the Executive Presbytery.[4]

- Churches lose an estimated 2,765,000 people each year to nominalism and secularism
- Between 3,500 to 4,000 churches close their doors each year in America
- Over the last ten years, the combined communicant membership of all Protestant denominations has declined by 9.5 percent (4,498,242), while national population has increased by 11 percent (24,253,000)
- Half of all churches last year did not add one new member through "conversion growth."

In a more recent paper by Dr. Dave Earley, director of church planting for Liberty University, July 17, 2006, *The Desperate Need for New Churches*, confirms these facts and adds that new churches are more effective at introducing people to Christ than existing churches.[5]

I would disagree with Dr. Earley in that existing churches can be just as effective as new churches but the existing church must make some obvious changes. At least they are obvious to those who feel that new churches are the answer.

The joy is that it can be changed. Just as God changes souls who give their life to Him, so can churches be born again. But just as we become a new creature, so must the church. It must align its mission with that of Christ and develop a new vision that focuses on His commandment to "Go into the world. Go everywhere and announce the Message of God's good news to one and all."

What Is The Worst Size Church?

The following is taken from PlusLine. PlusLine provides ministry support to Seventh-day Adventist church members, pastors, and church leaders throughout the North American Division. As the official helpdesk for general church information, PlusLine's duties include the collection and transmission of data related to nurture, or spiritual growth and outreach ministry.

> Like the human body, every church eventually plateaus. Its presence and impact are increased only by producing energetic offspring. A stunning statistic that illustrates the point: the average size of a five-year-old Southern Baptist church is 145 members. The average size of a 100-year-old Southern Baptist church is 155 members. Since these numbers are similar in Adventism, it is natural to wonder, why does it take 95 years to add ten members?[6]

The North American Mission Board, a division of the Southern Baptist Church, reported on May 1, 2006 that mid-sized churches (100-299) are shrinking while small and large churches are growing.[7] This is the worst possible size for successful continued growth. Getting past this milestone should be planned for early in the development of a church and every effort must be made to get past it quickly. This is the major obstacle for existing churches that are developing strategies for growth. There are physical, emotional, and spiritual problems associated with this size church. I have personally experienced these and still bear the scars to prove it.

Physical Obstacle

Let's consider a church with one hundred fifty regular attendees. Actual enrollment, although generally much larger, is usually worthless because it rarely accurately reflects the ability of the church to minister, nor does it properly reveal the growth attitude of the congregation.

What do the one hundred fifty regular attendees represent? First let's remove the infants, children, and teenagers. That reduction will not be proportionate to a much larger church because a church that has leveled off and is dying usually does not have a large group of younger attendees. Let's settle however on a figure of a hundred remaining adults out of one hundred fifty. Now let's remove those who are elderly and unable to help with the administration, instruction, and upkeep of the physical plant. At this point, we are reduced to approximately seventy-five adults who can actually perform the administration, instruction, and upkeep of the physical plant. Although these are also the ones who support a significant part of the needs of the church, they are not the majority of the financial givers. That usually comes from a very small group of folks over age fifty-five.[8]

So what is expected from these seventy-five people?

Administration:
Personnel matters
Planning and executing activities
Ordering materials
Fulfilling committee and board duties
Visitation
Ushering
Music ministry
Fund-raising

Instruction:
Five to seven adult Sunday school classes
Two to three teenage classes
Four to six children's classes
Two or more individuals for a nursery

Upkeep of the Physical Plant:
Cleaning the church
Mowing the lawn
Plumbing
Painting
General repairs
Cleaning gutters

If we use the 20 percent rule, meaning that 20 percent of the people do 80 percent of the work in most churches, there are about fifteen people doing all of the above tasks not seventy-five. That leads to emotional stress and eventual burnout.

Emotional Obstacle

As strong as many of us think we are, there are limits to our super-Christian endurance. At some point, even if you keep showing up, you are going to become ineffective. The simple fact is that many churches stop growing because all of their resources and abilities are consumed in maintaining the basic needs of the church. They realize that if they do not at least maintain what they have, they cannot afford to keep the absolute necessities such as a full time pastor. This maintenance effort can be extremely stressful to a church, even all-consuming. Of itself, maintenance is not a bad thing, but when it becomes the sole priority, it is very destructive. The only reason that maintenance can be good is that it means there is still a pulse and the church—the members—are still there, waiting on their leaders to catch a glimpse of a better approach. The end result of this maintenance-only approach is to expect the pastor to do the entire spiritual mission of the church. This attitude creates an atmosphere for failure. The emotional drain also creates hard feelings and drives wedges between otherwise logical individuals. Everyone is working so hard rowing the boat that they fail to see the waterfall dead ahead. At the bottom of that waterfall are the remains of thousands of well intending church folks who were so weary they were looking at the paddle instead of the horizon.

Spiritual Obstacle

The absence of spiritual growth is usually at the root of every small church's decline and ultimate failure. Failure to grow spiritually is the symptom, not the base cause. When maintenance is at the core of a church's ministry effort, there is no time for growth, whether physical or spiritual. For instance, when a teacher remains in a children's teaching position for an extended period of time without returning to an adult study, growth cannot occur without an extraordinary effort on the part of the teacher. In addition, many teachers accept that the most spiritual instruction they will receive is the weekly sermon. Not to diminish the role of the pastor or their sermons, but this is hardly where spiritual growth takes place, nor should it be. Look at the ministry of Christ. His disciples grew most from the one-on-one instruction from the teacher. It grew from their discussions with each other and those to whom Christ ministered. They were rarely idle when He was preaching; rather, they were ministering. Christ knew that, which is why he drew them aside. Learning, and therefore spiritual growth, will rarely come from a lecture, regardless of how entertaining or instructional it may be. The fallback in most of these instances is the pastor. The total responsibility for spiritual growth is laid at the feet of the pastor. In addition, the pastor is loaded with the responsibility for sermons, mid-week Bible study, visiting the sick, weddings, funerals, and a few administrative duties.

In a maintenance based ministry the goal is to fill positions. Unfortunately, the first thought that comes into a congregation's mind when new members join the church is the empty positions the new member can fill. The first thought should be how the body of Christ, the church, can help these people grow by discovering their gifts and then providing an opportunity for them to use those gifts outside the church as well as inside.

If a church is to grow, the church cannot turn every opportunity inward, which is what maintenance requires. This is the result of getting stuck in the worst possible sized congregation. This is why many, if not most churches, remain at exactly the size that demands maintenance ministry. So, what are the excuses used to justify remaining small? Let's explore a few.

Two

So How Do Churches Remain Small?

"Where Two or Three Are Gathered Together…"

In the book of Matthew, we find only two references to the word *church*, one of which doesn't even use the word church. Matthew 16:18 speaks of the universal church: "You are Peter, a rock. This is the rock on which I will put together my church, a church so expansive with energy that not even the gates of hell will be able to keep it out." In Matthew 18:20 we find the statement, "For where two or three are gathered together in my name, there am I in the midst of them." This last reference, often taken out of context, is used to support a small group's reason for existence. It is unfairly used as an excuse for the fact that there has been no spiritual or physical growth.

Looking at the scripture, it is important to note that it does not refer to the actions taken by a few to gather together, rather, it says that they are *gathered*. So what is the difference? First, it is important to look at the entire passage. This passage follows one of the most important church discipline instructions found in the Bible—Matthew 18:15-17. "If a fellow believer hurts you, go and tell him—work it out between the two of you. If he listens, you've made a friend. If he won't listen, take one or two others along so that the presence of witnesses will keep things honest, and try again. If he still won't listen, tell the church. If he won't listen to the church, you'll have to start over from scratch, confront him with the need for repentance, and offer again God's forgiving love." If this instruction were followed, there would be beautiful harmony within the church. This is a passage that defines reconciliation, one of the most important doctrines of the Christian faith. Instead of recognizing this doctrine, some churches today choose to ignore the instruction in verse fifteen and use the "two or three" concept in verse twenty to justify their failure to obey Christ's command to bring others to Him. This earlier verse, Matthew 18:15, gives us an outline to follow when we are wronged or when a disagreement arises within the church.

Second, Matthew 18:20 speaks of a name that has the authority to gather us. We should feel His calling to service. That should be the reason we are together, not because we like the church, the building, the people, the name, the music, the preacher, or anything else. His gathering two or three to work through a problem using His outline is not justification for the fact that we have not ventured outside the church to minister to the needs of our community and provide the tools necessary for a world to make a decision about their relationship with Christ. It is at that point of decision, of developing a relationship with Christ, that they begin to feel called to be gathered together. They should also begin to feel His call to ministry and mission. If they do not, the church has most likely not provided immediate opportunities for these new converts to discover their abilities and offer a ministry *outside* the church that can utilize those gifts. Anything short of that process is maintenance, and maintenance is synonymous with failure.

Numbers Do Not Matter

Numbers may not be an acceptable method of measuring success in a church, but the absence of them will surely measure failure. Countless times I have overheard people discuss a nongrowth church and say, with pious fortitude, that numbers should never be used to measure the effectiveness of a church. Some would go so far as to say that you should not count heads and report attendance. They hold that if the church introduces one soul to the Kingdom, the church has done what it should and will be blessed. This is nothing more than an excuse. The church does not introduce people to the Lord. *People* introduce people to the Lord. That puts a new face on this discussion. If the church does not introduce people to the Lord, what is the church's purpose? Good question. We will get to that later. First though, let's look at numbers.

Where should we begin? Perhaps in Numbers, the book in the Old Testament, the *begat* book. Why was it necessary to put that book in the Bible? That book has prevented more people from reading through the Bible than I could count. The book was necessary for definition. The book wastes no time: He said, "Number the congregation of the People of Israel by clans and families, writing down the names of every male" (Numbers 1:2). We needed to understand how God did His work and His way of measuring that work.

If God had said in the beginning that there would be someone who would come that would crush the head of the serpent (Genesis 3:15) and then there was no way to document that, how would we know if it were true? In that same passage there are numerous other instances of counting, beginning with, "In the beginning." Why did God count the days? Why not just say, He made the earth? Then there is birth, murder, the casting out of Cain, followed by more counting. Genesis 4:17 begins a lineage of Cain's descendents. In Genesis 4:25, Seth is born, and the book begins to outline the lineage of his offspring as well.

Why is it important in Genesis 5:3–5 to tell us how old Adam was on three different occasions? Later in this same chapter, the author gives a listing of ages of each of the individuals as it did for Adam and Seth. Why was that important? Note the beginning of verse one in Genesis 6: "When men began to increase in number…" So what does this have to do with counting in the modern day church? Everything.

"Our preacher is so conscience of numbers. He always talks about how many we had at church." "I know there were only five at prayer meeting, but numbers don't matter; the ones that were there were blessed." "There was just a handful at the revival, but the messages were delightful, and we were all blessed." These are comforting statements. These are the things we tell ourselves to mask the disappointment that we are not growing; however, if the numbers increase, suddenly the attitude changes. Suddenly numbers are our friend, and we want to tell everyone. It is only when our numbers are decreasing that we look for comfort, or worse, excuses.

"Our attendance has fallen way off; it must be the preacher." "Giving is way down; what did we do to offend people?" It seems as long as we can maintain the status quo, we are complacently satisfied. When numbers drop though, suddenly they are important. Time after time in the scriptures there are accountings of people. The accounts of Abraham were numbered. The Exodus of Moses was counted. As you continue on in the Old Testament, the writers count. Moving into the New Testament, the trend does not change. Jesus fed five thousand with three loaves and two fishes. There were counted among them three thousand who were saved at Pentecost. Revelation is packed with purposeful numbers.

Sometimes I do not like to look in my checkbook because I do not want to be reminded that I am broke. Sometimes we do not like to discuss numbers in the church because it reminds us that we are a diminishing asset; unless we can replace ourselves, one day the doors of our church will surely close. The next time you sing the song, "Count Your Blessings," point to each person sitting around you. They are your blessings. They are the ones that God has spoken to and commanded to evangelize the lost. Then point to yourself. It must start with you! Don't wait on everyone else to introduce someone to the Lord. Start counting the ones you introduce. That's how the church grows. That's how it works. God counts. In fact, He keeps a book, and your name should be in it.

An Accounting

God has given us a plan just as He gave one to all His people throughout the Bible. We must be measured. How else can we know that we are accomplishing His purpose? There are many other documented accounts in the scriptures—too many to discuss here. There is one, however, that I feel we need to note, because it is key to understanding this question of nongrowth in our society as it relates to churches. We find this statement in the book of Acts, the birthplace of the modern church.

"Those who accepted his message were baptized, and about three thousand were added to their number that day" (Acts 2:41). Why was it necessary to record this passage in the most important section of our heritage? Simply, it showed that there was response. Not just a response, but a significant response. What if there had been just one who responded? Would it have been recorded? Maybe so, but what would the impact have been? Would it have appeared to be the beginning of a movement? Probably not.

The end of Acts 2:47 is a chilling statement when applied to modern churches that have not grown: "And the Lord added to their number daily those who were being saved." When a church goes for weeks, months, and in some cases years with no one giving their life to Christ, it should send a signal to the leadership of the church. It should bother the pastor. While the church does exist in part for that one unsaved individual in church who keeps procrastinating, this ministry does not excuse the body of Christ from searching their community for many more who need to hear His message.

However, the problem may not be that folks are not being saved and added daily, or at least weekly, but that they *are* being saved, joining the fellowship for a short period and then jumping ship when they discover there is nothing else. Have they been saved into a maintenance congregation?

The Country Club

Sometimes these maintenance churches are called by another name—country clubs. Ouch, that hurts, you say. It was said in our church in a leadership meeting. Many took offence, but upon reflection, they agreed that the description fit. In fact, we were not even a good country club. Our dues were not high enough! In addition, we had very little expectation that members would even pay them.

What characterizes the benefits of a country club? A short list might contain the comfortable life, greens maintenance, status within the community, a member in good standing, providing programs and features for the expectations of the membership, and dues. One thing you will not find at the top of most country clubs priority list: service to others outside the club. In fact, other than an occasional fund-raiser for a high profile charity, there is no expectation to provide services to those outside the club, only to satisfy the members' needs. If outsiders do come in, they must do it through one of the members and usually at an increased cost called a guest fee. So how does that contrast with what a church should be? The quote in the beginning of this book sums up why a church, any church, should exist, "The church is the only organization that exists for the benefit of its non-members," said William Temple, former Arch Bishop of Canterbury.

Think about your church. What are the top three ministries of your church, and where and to whom are they directed? Is your worship service designed to satisfy the needs of those who attend regularly, or is it designed to meet the needs of a community who may not know anything about Christ or the church? What about Sunday school? Are the classes designed to meet the needs of those who attend regularly, or are they designed to meet the needs of those who know nothing about Christ and His church in their community? What about your youth ministry? Is it designed to accommodate the children of adult members, or is it designed to meet the needs of kids in the community whose parents, if they exist, do not attend church? What about your men's and women's groups?

Are they designed to do maintenance on the facility and minister to those within your congregation, or do they exist to go into the community and the world and help those less fortunate rebuild their homes and churches after disasters? Are those groups designed and intentionally motivated to minister to those in your community and bring them to the church to learn about a better way of life and the One who provides it? What percent of your offerings are spent on in-church ministry as opposed to outreach?

Here is an interesting exercise. Do a search on the internet for the percentage of married individuals who attend church. The obvious percentage that remains is those who are not married. These folks could be divorced, never married, too young to marry, or those who have lost their spouse and will never remarry. You should find in your research that about 59 percent of those who attend church are married. Now ask yourself this question regarding your current ministries. Do 41 percent of our ministries intentionally provide needed support and education to those who are single? Next, search to find a list of the top ten reasons people get a divorce. Look at those reasons and determine how many of those reasons are being intentionally addressed by your church, not just your pastor. True ministry is what was given by example by Christ while walking among people. He went to the people where they were. He became interested in their specific needs. He addressed those needs and wrapped them in His love and example.

Is your church a country club? Don't be too proud to say yes. It's a start.

Retention

I belong to a large industry association. One of the most important chairmen in that organization is called the *retention chair*. This person is charged with the responsibility of keeping people in the organization. If the association adds six hundred members in a year but loses seven hundred, there is no gain. In fact, the association is in decline. To keep members, the association has to provide value through education, political influence, and networking about new industry ideas among other things. After receiving these services, the members are expected to then recruit new members who will in turn benefit from the same services offered to the original member. How does this apply to the church? Answer this question by taking an honest look at your church. In the past ten years how many people have come into your fellowship, and how many of them are still there? That is how you calculate retention.

Your church may be providing all of the things that are needed for those who come into the church. However, if the participants are not maturing spiritually from that experience and introducing others to Christ, there is a problem. It may be that your church is not offering the right things that are needed for spiritual growth. As within many of the churches I have visited, it may be that there is simply no expectation to grow. There could be many things that are not working correctly. The challenge for today's nongrowth church is to be honest with themselves, admit that there is a spiritual problem, and then, with God's guidance, set out to discover what is not working. It is only then that growth can begin. Only then can the church record, as it did in Acts 2:47, that "People in general liked what they saw. Every day their number grew as God added those who were saved."

Three Types of New Members

All churches experience three types of new members: new Christians, newborns, and movers. The last in this list can be a heart breaker and a church splitter. Although churches may grow in three ways, they also shrink in a variety of ways. The early church experienced growth through the first two. That is why their growth was sustained. These are, in their purest form, true growth. However if your church growth model consists of waiting on folks to walk in to your church, well, that constitutes waiting on a miracle.

The first type of growth mentioned above, new Christians, is a result of following Christ's commandment to go into all the world and introduce others to Him. This is evangelism, pure and simple. It is also an effort to get outside the walls of the sanctuary and do something. Most church growth comes from members asking another person to join them. It may not be an invitation to worship, but rather to a small group, a Sunday school class, a dinner, or a ballgame. It may just be for a walk, or even, heaven help us, a game of golf at the country club—the real country club. This interaction takes effort, courage, and preparation. It also takes spiritual growth, leadership by the Holy Spirit, and discernment—three things missing in most nongrowth churches. Courage comes from framing these three elements within a life of faith. There is a difference between spirituality and spiritual growth. Too often spirituality is considered a place, a noun. It should be a verb, an action. Spiritual growth is a journey. A journey where, the farther you go, the more you realize you need directions. A growing church will know how to provide those directions, and they do not lead to the sanctuary. They lead to the street.

The second type of growth is natural, newborns. People have children, and those children grow up. Many of them accept Christ and join the fellowship. Many of them, however, do not stay. They are lost for several reasons, but here are four that stand out.

- They go off to college and never get back to their original church; if they get back to church at all.
- They reach the age of maturity and decide not to attend anymore.
- They reach the donut hole, the part that is missing, the age where the church forgot to provide ministry, thinking that the young person would magically morph from a high school senior into an old person in the blink of an eye.
- They marry someone of another faith or no faith at all.

Natural growth is not predictable, as illustrated above, and generally works against positive growth if that is the major tool used to sustain the church. Ironically, in growing churches, this type of growth is a leading contributor to growth. Why? There is no donut hole. Ministry is continuous from cradle to grave. These churches do not accept the fact that young people dropping out of church is just the way it is. Hard isn't it? Not really.

The third group is worth a lot of discussion, *the movers*. When I first started in sales I was warned about folks who called and wanted to buy insurance. They probably needed it for something that had already happened, or they would not qualify. Sometimes after meeting and trying to work with some of these church movers, I wondered if they were the same ones who called me for insurance. Let me first say that there are exceptions. Some folks, because of a job change, buying a new home in another community, or legitimate disagreement with their previous church's theology or direction are forced to find another church home. This latter group is generally an asset to their new church family. The mere fact that they took the time to find a new church home shows that they are dedicated to Christ's cause. But then there are the movers, the folks who became upset over some petty matter at their previous church and moved to yours.

After a brief honeymoon with their new church, a familiar phrase is heard from the lips of a mover, "Let me tell you how we did it at the last church I belonged too." Did you ever wonder why they left if everything was so perfect at the other place? Although a lot could be said about this group, it probably shouldn't because it would all be negative. That is exactly what a nongrowth church needs to avoid. Just let it be said that if you are intentionally trying to grow your church through the first step, following Christ's commandment, this third group will take care of itself. When there is spiritual growth present, immaturity sticks out like a sore thumb. A positive attitude in a church is contagious; unfortunately, so in negativism.

I believe churches remain small because there is nothing to suggest to them that something is wrong. There is a failure to connect to the truth about why they exist. Churches remain small because there is an element of comfort in just maintaining the status quo.

At the end of the day, a small church is who they are because of every decision they have made as individuals, pastor included, since their birth as a church. In his book, *Seven Practices of Effective Ministry*, Andy Stanley makes the following statement, "Your ministry is perfectly designed to achieve the results you are currently getting."[9] Well-said Andy.

The only worse example to the world, other than a nongrowth church, is a church that once had a great ministry, but through moral corruption, pride, unresolved differences, bitterness, pettiness, unresolved theology, or other internal problems declined to small church status and never recovered. Remember my definition of a small church, "I believe *any* church is small that is not actively, intentionally focusing on God's call to ministry."

Consider Matthew 5:14—16. "You are the light of the world. A city on a hill cannot be hidden. Neither do people light a lamp and put it under a bowl. Instead they put it on its stand, and it gives light to everyone in the house. In the same way, let your light shine before men, that they may see your good deeds and praise your Father in heaven." When did the lights go out in the little brown church? Were they ever turned on? Were they on, and the curtains blocked their light? These are valid questions with so many nongrowth churches spread across our countryside's. Many may not want to think about it, but somebody has to bring this up. God is waiting; it's your turn to convince Him that it is okay. I'm just the messenger. Please don't shoot me.

Three

Why Did The Lights Go Out?

Were They Ever On?

In answer to the question raised in the title of this section, yes the lights have been on for a very long time. There was a bright light shining in the early days of our country. However, the torch burned for a different reason. While it was important to preach the gospel to all who would listen, and introducing souls to the Lord was always the central theme, the burning desire was for religious freedom, breaking the bounds of the organized church in England. If you have read the New Testament, this should sound familiar.

That passion led to more than religious freedom. A possibly unintended outcome was the birth of a new nation. That passion for breaking away from the religious norm created a nation where anyone can worship the way they feel is appropriate. There are very few places on the face of the earth where that can be done. In fact, there are still places were that action will end your life and possibly, those of your family, as well. So what happened? Where did that spirit go? With all that sacrifice and passion in our history, how can those involved in modern, small churches be satisfied with the status quo? How can maintenance be the priority of the small church, or any church, when over half of the American population, not to mention billions of others on this planet, do not know the freedom that comes in serving Christ? This is an interesting question and one that needs to be addressed.

A Light on a Hill Cannot Be Hidden

Remember the scripture quoted in an earlier chapter, Matthew 5:14—16. "You are the light of the world. A city on a hill cannot be hidden. Neither do people light a lamp and put it under a bowl. Instead they put it on its stand, and it gives light to everyone in the house. In the same way, let your light shine before men, that they may see your good deeds and praise your Father in heaven." The metaphor *light* may not be the key word. Maybe the word we need to concentrate on is *hill*.

The church in America, whether small, medium, or large, is set apart. Even those who do not believe in the church recognize it as an important influence in our culture. They also hold the church to a higher standard. If a politician goes bad it is expected, but let the clergy go bad, and it is just not acceptable. The politician is replaced, and the world goes on. Let the church mess up, and it takes years to overcome, if it ever does.

Yes, the church is set on a hill. The church is being observed, even if, as related in the popular song, "From a distance," written by Julie Gold and made popular by Bette Midler. The world knows when the lights are on or off. The motel advertisement that says, "We'll leave the light on for ya", is a perfect example of how we need to be viewed by the world. Nothing is more beautiful to someone who is lost in a dark forest than to see, way off in the distance, a small faint light. They assume that someone is there at that light source. They may not know who it is or what they will find, but there is *hope*. What if, when they reach the light, they find the same innkeeper who was in Bethlehem? What if they find the one who informed Mary and Joseph that there was no room in the inn.

Another verse comes to mind, similar to the one above. Luke

11:33—35 says, "No one lights a lamp, then hides it in a drawer. It's put on a lamp stand so those entering the room have light to see where they're going." Then in verse 36, "Your eye is a lamp, lighting up your whole body. If you live wide-eyed in wonder and belief, your body fills up with light. If you live squinty-eyed in greed and distrust, your body is a dank cellar. Keep your eyes open, your lamp burning, so you don't get musty and murky. Keep your life as well-lighted as your best-lighted room."

In verse 33, the scripture refers to a drawer used to hide the light. A lamp is intended to give light to those immediately around the lamp. A lamp is useless outside. Its light is not directed like a flashlight, but gives off a warm light that illuminates those who are close. If the world sees the faint light from far off and comes close only to find that those who control the lamp are unwilling to share that light, what does that say? It says that those who control the lamp are, contrary to Jesus' teaching, unwilling to share that light of love. You may say that your church would never refuse to share the love held within your control. You would never refuse to love someone who came into your church. That may be the point; they have to come into your church. Why not take the light (love) to them? Why not walk boldly into your neighborhood, holding the lamp high above your head? Then when they do come to the light do you move over and let them pull up to the warmth of the light beside you, or did they have to squeeze in and make room for themselves? This scripture brings some very deep and troubling questions to the table of churches with no growth, questions that must be asked and addressed.

Matthew 11 also refers to the eyes being the lamp of our body. Verse 36 speaks of the *whole* body. This could also be a metaphor of the church. It talks about the whole body being full of light. That means everyone within the body of Christ, sometimes referred to as the bride of Christ, the church. God's intent for us as individuals is to keep our light on. When we come together as a church, regardless of size, he expects that everyone will combine their lamps and put them on a tower, a tower that sits on a hill in the middle of a light starved world. If, on a clear night, a single match can be seen over a mile away, at what distance could a lost soul see three hundred matches? What about just twenty? What about one blow torch created by a dynamic growing church!?

The eye is an amazing organ. There is a theory, recognized by many noted scientists, called *irreducible complexity* that suggests that the eye is so complex that it could not have evolved from a simpler life form, refuting Darwinian evolution and pointing to an intelligent designer. Because of that complexity, the longer an eye sits in total darkness, the more it is able to see with less light.[10] Similarly, someone who has been in the depths of sin and depression, totally blind because of the darkness that surrounds their world, could pick up the faintest light of hope from the church. Unfortunately, statistics show us that there is not enough light coming from many churches to be seen, even in total darkness. Why? We will attempt to answer that question in later chapters of this book. Finding an answer is not optional. There are millions who are out there right now bumping into unknown obstacles in total darkness. They deserve hope. Should not the church be willing to share their hope with the world? I think Christ would say, you bet!

Ran out of Lamp Oil

There are many reasons why the small church's lights may not be on. Maybe they just ran out of lamp oil. Any light needs fuel. What is that fuel? The scripture clearly tells us that Jesus said, "I am the Road, also the Truth, also the Life. No one gets to the Father apart from me. If you really knew me, you would know my Father as well. From now on, you do know him. You've even seen him!" John 14:6-7. Anyone who follows Him will have eternal life. In John 1:3—5 we are told that, "Everything was created through him; nothing—not one thing!—came into being without him. What came into existence was Life, and the Life was Light to live by. The Life-Light blazed out of the darkness; the darkness couldn't put it out." This act of not understanding tells us that simply having the light initially is not sufficient. It becomes our expected duty to explain that light to those who have seen it. However, how can we explain something that we have not taken the time to learn? What is the barrier? Possibly, the missing fuel is simply a lack of spiritual growth.

We are given the light, the light that is in Him when we accept Him as our Lord and Savior. That light will always be bright enough for us to see our way, but without spiritual growth our light becomes useless to the world around us—as useless as a small lamp in a dark, stormy night. Churches of any size that are turned inward, doing just enough to get by, are closing the shutters over their windows and blocking the life-giving light that was intended for the world.

Did Not Trim the Wicks

Another possibility is that churches have failed to trim their wicks. When a candle is allowed to burn for a long period of time, the wax around the wick melts faster than the wick burns. There is a carbon deposit that accumulates at the tip of the wick called a *mushroom*. The wick gets its fuel from the mixture in the wax. If the candle burns down faster than the wick, the wick becomes its own source of fuel. There are two problems with this. First, the mushroom prohibits the wick from properly combining the burning wax and surrounding oxygen. Second, the material in the wick will burn away. If the wick is not trimmed, the light will dim and if not corrected over a long period of time, the light will simply go out, even with an adequate supply of fuel.

What about the wicks in your church? Are you trimming them? Do you understand why they should be trimmed? There is an old saying that has stood the test of time: If you always do what you always do, you will always get what you always get. Left unaltered, the habits of a church will eventually turn out the lights. Part of that wick trimming may involve pruning programs that have been in place for years. They may be stifling needed growth from other programs. Furthermore, as we journey through life, experiences and human nature will naturally cover us with a residue of sin and neglect. You cannot help get it on you. Over time those layers of residue will extinguish our light if we do not clean up occasionally — preferably daily. Our effectiveness will decrease with the intensity of our light. To the world, it may even appear that the lights are out. If we are not getting the proper combination of fuel (His word) and oxygen (spiritual training), we are going to become ineffective as the instruments we were intended to be. If we as individuals are ineffective, the churches that we represent will likewise become useless. That, unfortunately, appears to be the state of many of our churches.

Dependent on Someone Else to Supply Fuel

What about your church? Do you expect the pastor to do all of the spiritual work? Do you wait on your denominational leaders to supply you with resources for a community in which they do not live? Are you as a layperson involved in developing and implementing ways of teaching and sending people out into the world to minister? Whose job is it to minister? Why is your church not growing? Does it bother you? Does it bother you enough to do something about it? Do you know what your gifts are? Are you using them? If you are, where and how are you using them? If the answer is, "in the church", please note the word *in*. Serving in the church, but not in the world could be the root cause of your dim light and therefore one of many weak links in your churches effort to brighten your ministry.

There are thousands of questions that can be asked. There are ten fingers that can be pointed in ten different directions to explain away the failure of the average denominational church to grow. One thing is certain. The answer and solution begins with you, not the church. Again, the church doesn't bring anyone to Christ, people do. He is not asking you to do anything He has not done Himself. It was one man who stood up to the leaders of the organized church.

It was one man who taught a small group of men who eventually taught thousands, who taught millions over the centuries. It was one man who took our scorn and punishment. It was one man who was beaten almost to death and then crucified. Until His death, he felt the same pain you feel. Praise God that He *overcame.* He invites you, one person, to do no less.

He has provided everything you need to be successful. He even supplied an instruction manual (the Bible) and a companion (the Holy Spirit) who serves as tour guide, coach, and counselor. Come on. Flip the switch. Turn the lights on! Better yet, grab the lamp and head out the door. You may be surprised who is attracted to your light and shows up at the door. Invite them in for a while or to take a walk with you. The church is a hospital, not a nursing home. People come to the church for healing, not as a place to die. As soon as they understand the light , don't send them out, take them out into the world and give them an opportunity to minister to folks who are in the same circumstances as they were before they saw your light. Now we are talking megawatts!

Is Church a Place to Hide?

Earlier I said that the church is not a place to die. Is it a place to hide?

The following is a litany of my frustrations with the world that, if allowed to dominate, will mess with my very predictable life. When I reach that overwhelming state of frustration all I want to do is hide.

Recently, there was yet another made-for-TV movie on cable. It had many of the standard Hollywood actors and actresses playing out a familiar plot involving catastrophic weather disasters that were expected to bring on the end of the world. Everything that the world has to offer or criticize was woven into this melodrama, including a slam on a big church, money-hungry evangelist and his wife. Sodom and Gomorrah had nothing on this made-for-TV world. I only watched one episode of the mini-series; it was all I could take. I wanted to give my TV away and isolate myself from such bad screenwriting. The plot, in part, blamed the end of the world on the organized church. Unfortunately there is a hungry world that watches this junk and believes it.

My occupation often places me in direct contact with state and federal politicians. The actions of many of these politicians are base; their language, when off the microphone, is unprofessional and deplorable. Many politicians, though certainly not the majority, are only interested in power and re-election. Some even find themselves in jail for their actions. Often, after returning from these interactions, I want to hide in the mountains of Oregon and never have contact with these individuals again.

I used to have a very old cell phone. The only thing the old cell phone could do was make and receive calls. It had been dropped several times and occasionally did not work very well. Even so, I found that I could not get away from it. If I forgot it, I felt like I had been disconnected from the planet. Something might have happened, and no one would have been able to call and tell me. So, what did I do? I got rid of it. Now I have one that receives email, connects me to the world-wide web, automatically connects to my car radio when I enter my vehicle, and reminds me that I am late for appointments; and yes it has a camera and a copy of the entire Bible in seven versions. Just one time, I would like to go on a trip, leave my phone at home, and not take a call until I return.

It disturbs me that right after I get used to my computer software, it changes, and every couple of years I have to learn all over again. I wish I could just keep using what I am used to.

My favorite sport is baseball. I still feel that Willie Mays and Mickey Mantle should be able to make a come back. I don't understand why there has to be a designated hitter in one of the leagues. I don't understand why most of the players on a winning World Series team all move the next year to another team. Why can't they just leave my game alone?

The cars I drive keep changing, and my clothes keep going out of style. I have forty-five RPM's, thirty-three 1/3 RPM LPs, 8-tracks, cassettes, CDs, DVDs, and even ".wav" files on my hard drive, and now an iPod. Why can't they just stop changing stuff? I want things to be the way they used to be.

If all of the above is such a big deal to me in my late fifties I can certainly understand why folks older than me just want the world to stop moving so fast. Unfortunately, there is nothing that seniors can do to stop the world and return things to the way they used to be. However, there is one place that has not changed for many of these folks. It is also a place where many of them have the ability to freeze time and remember how it used to be. It is a place to say to a younger generation that this is how you are supposed to do things. It is actually a really great place to hide. It is the average American church. No one can blame these folks for wanting the world to slow down. The problem is that this is not natural. Things are meant to change. We should listen to the scripture if we are looking for a place to hide. "Keep your eye on me; hide me under your cool wing feathers from the wicked who are out to get me, from mortal enemies closing in." (Psalm 17:8-9). "That's the only quiet, secure place in a noisy world, the perfect getaway, far from the buzz of traffic." (Psalm 27:5).

The quiet, secure place in the previous scripture is not referring to the church building. This concept rang clear to me recently while I was visiting the Mayan ruins in Tulum on the East coast of Mexico, near the Yucatan Peninsula. Our tour guide was explaining the Mayan temple when he used the two phrases *holy place* and *holiest place*. He mentioned that everyone could go into the holy place, but only the pure could enter the holiest. On my return bus trip to the ship, it occurred to me that after Christ came, and the curtain in the temple was torn in two, that the holist place is now my heart, the place where Christ lives. Although the church building may be a holy place, Christ does not live there. Therefore, I cannot hide in the building. The church is not a place to hide, but a place to be open and filled with the light of Christ. That light should shine from the hearts of those whose holiest-of-holy hearts gather there for worship. That worship should be to celebrate their ministry from the past week, to gain encouragement from others who have experienced and overcome difficulty, and to launch the future week's ministry. The gathering should never be to simply proclaim *once* a week that "Jesus lives." Most everyone at the church has heard that countless times. It's the world that needs the message.

Be Still and Know That I Am God

Every year at our annual passion play, there is a piece of unintended humor at the very beginning of the presentation. The audience is sitting in complete darkness, and it is so quiet, you can hear the audience breathing. A Roman soldier appears from nowhere, slams his spear against the wooden stage and shouts, "Quiet!" This, I believe, is a picture of the modern day church, all denominations included. I have heard the scripture, "Be still, and know that I am God; I will be exalted among the nations, I will be exalted in the earth", from Psalm 46:10 (NIV version) quoted time after time in respect to forms of worship, educational processes, and denominational publications, all of which directly affect the future ability of these churches to be God's tool for ministry. This verse is certainly taken out of context when the church is already so quiet that you can hear it breathing and can literally feel the heartbeat of a frightened people.

The problem may be that we have been quiet, heard the voice of the Lord, and didn't like what we heard. There is always a certain assurance in doing nothing. At least we don't make mistakes when we do nothing. Maybe we should look to the Heavens and shout, PRAISE THE LORD! Maybe we need to look to the Heavens and stop making excuses for our inaction. There are instances when the Lord told His Leaders to be silent and let Him show his glory. Such a time came during the exodus of His people from Egypt. That incident, however, was a singular event. The rest of the time, God told Moses to act, to get up and go. Don't ask questions; just follow.

There have been times in history when churches have followed such orders either through obedience or necessity. For Cumberland Presbyterians, a small denomination that began after disagreements with the regular Presbyterian Church in 1810, their most dramatic growth was right after the new denomination's formation. Very few churches today enjoy growth at the same rate as that initial growth. What happened?

The Cumberland Presbyterian Church, and other denominations that came out of the period, known as the second great awakening, looked a lot more like the churches of today that are growing and introducing others to Christ. Today, most of the Cumberland Presbyterian Church's ministries, teaching, evangelism, and worship style don't look anything like their original model. Comparatively, these growing, nondenominational churches are the ones that have passed from the *be still* stage to the *let's get it done* stage. Today's denominational churches may have to stop the rhetoric about not conforming to the world. They might have to stop using their reluctance to becoming a part of the Pentecostal movement as an excuse for doing nothing but keeping Sunday school classes staffed and a minister in the pulpit. Instead, it may be time that we stopped conforming to the rituals of the denominational church established by man. I am not speaking about the sacraments or the message of Jesus Christ, but all of the other stuff; rituals, dress code and legalism.

Consider Christ in the garden. He was quiet. He was seeking God's will in His earthly life. In His quietness, He was not still, but moved with deep compassion for His mission. So much was this the case that His sweat fell like great drops of blood. After His prayer, His listening, His stillness, came action. From that moment on, His life was filled with purpose even though it was surrounded by constant noise and confusion. He could have retreated and kept quiet. Aren't you glad he didn't? So, am I suggesting that the Cumberland Presbyterian Church and her sister denominations become a Trinity Broadcasting Network look-alike? Far from it. We can, however, learn from those brothers and sisters. They have figured out that what used to work doesn't anymore. They have two issues that they talk about a lot: evangelism and money. The first you say is worthy while the second is entirely inappropriate. Oh really? First, why isn't our main focus on either one of these? Second, what have we done so well that allows us to criticize? Let me suggest a few changes we could make in addition to rethinking how we address money and evangelism:

- Open up our worship services to a more inclusive style. I'm not just talking about race; I'm talking about worship that reflects the lives of a contemporary community with multiple generational needs.
- Use more music (not more hymns) that speaks of praise and worship in the twenty-first century.
- Use more instruments in all worship services than piano and organ, and not just the worship service attended by the youth.
- Include more people in the presentation of the service.
- Have testimonies, praise times, and an occasional sermon that is not read.
- Change the scenery. Maybe it is time to paint the paneling and move the pulpit to the other side of the stage. Yes, change! There, I said it. As hard as it may be, I did say the "C" word.
- Change the order of worship; maybe even extend the service to an hour and fifteen minutes to accommodate the additional participation. You might want to watch who objects to this one. You might just look for an opportunity for discussion. God did not ordain that the worship must consist of one hour services complete with piano and organ accompaniment, choir robes, bulletins, coats and ties, doxologies, and a special before the sermon and out the door in time for lunch.

If we are to hold on to security blankets, should we not be expected to identify what we consider to be the problem and offer solutions that will positively effect the growth patterns of our churches? Let me issue a challenge to our pastors. Please don't be the Roman soldier banging his spear on the wooden floor and screaming, "Quiet!" I beg you to raise holy hands and shout, "Praise the Lord!" Other than losing your job, it can't hurt. Think about it.

Why Is This Important?

Why is it important that nondenominational churches grow? Our world cannot afford to lose the impact of millions of Christians who make up the denominational world. It would be like changing from gasoline to ethanol overnight. A sudden change like that could crush our economy. Likewise for all denominations to close their doors suddenly would be devastating to the Christian base in this Country. Humanity doesn't change that fast. In addition, the denominational structure is not the problem. There is just as much structure in a nondenominational church; it is just held closer to the vest. The problem is that the denominational structure has become something it was never intended to be—a legalistic substitute for personal spiritual growth. Denominations need to fix the problem, not reinvent themselves. I trust that our nondenominational brothers and sisters would agree. After all, they are not in existence to put denominations out of business. They are currently doing denominational churches a favor by accomplishing what denominations seem to have no desire to attempt—growth. Nondenominational churches are filling the void left by thousands of denominational churches across America that, at one time, were the backbone of our country's moral fiber. Am I suggesting that denominational churches are not moral? No. They are, however, for the most part, weak, lifeless, and hardly a challenge to the godless agenda we face every day. I might add that a few denominational churches speaking out in the media on social and moral issues do not resolve the larger problem. The way we fight these issues is by training Christians in our churches and in our homes so that when challenged by the world at work, at school or in other secular settings, they are spiritually mature enough to fight. A church that is so busy keeping teachers in classrooms and paying the bills cannot be expected to be on the front line of Christ's battle to win the hearts of the world.

I could have easily filled this book with boring facts and details about the decline of the modern church and Christianity in America. You can find that information as well as I can. Let's just agree that there is a serious problem and work together to fix it. I promise that the last part of this book will give you tools that will raise blisters on your hands, if you will use them, those blisters will achieve the results you have been praying for.

Four

Denominational or Nondenominational

The subtitle of this book is, "A look at the dying twenty-first century denominational movement and maybe its last hope. It is time we identify the problem and offer a solution."

We often judge circumstances by our inability to handle them or understanding where the circumstances originate. The influence of a denominational structure often is the unwritten source of our problems as laypersons. The most powerful effect that a denomination has is its intentional impact on the pastorate. As in the following example, influence can have an emotional and lasting impact.

A few years ago, one of our younger members approached me in my position as an elder and wanted to know why our church was having such a hard time handling change. She had occasionally attended another large, nondenominational church in our community and, unlike our very denominationally directed church, noted that they had grown continuously over the years. She also noted that it was always a very positive, happy place to worship. By the time she finished talking and asking questions, during which time I had yet to open my mouth, she was crying. She was judging our church and our members' inability to handle the circumstances based on her previous church experiences. She never really brought denominationalism into the discussion. Why? Because to her, it was transparent, without any regard to denominations or any other structure. She was not steeped in traditions, especially, in this case, Cumberland Presbyterian. However at its core, denominationalism is very much an issue with the problem of church growth, not because there is a problem with denominations in and of themselves, but because most denominations have turned inward and boarded up all of the outside windows.

We have had denominations from the beginning. After Cain slew Abel, there was the family of Cain, the Canaanites. Many years later came the well-known twelve tribes of Israel. Denominations began as families, a term churches love to use today. The Gaithers' even wrote their version of the popular secular tune "We Are Family" sung by *Sister Sledge* in 1979. The Gaither's version was called, "The Family of God." Denominations may have started as families, but modern denominations have developed very different internal structures, many of which are rigid and unchangeable. If you are in the middle of this fray, take heart; Jesus faced the same organized church. He was crucified for His stance. That makes your contemporary troubles seem a bit trivial don't you think?

Today, there are three accepted forms of church government. First, although Catholics and Episcopalians would not consider themselves part of denominations, they are groups of individuals with similar beliefs run by a particular form of church government that utilizes an appointed Pope and priest or bishop. A second form of church government in which the congregation elects elders to perform the business and operation of the church is Presbyterian. This form is very similar to the structure of our United States Congress. After all, many of the founding members were Presbyterian. In short, Catholics have a Pope and priests, Episcopalians have bishops, and Presbyterians have elders. How are the Baptists, Pentecostals, Church of Christ, and several other denominations run? This third form of government is called *congregational,* theoretically run by the congregation.

Why were these denominations and various forms of church

government formed? There are many more reasons than this book could possibly address. In general, however, people of like minds like to stick together. Additionally, there are theological reasons why different groups were formed, and then after additional disagreements, these re-formed groups divided again. On a side note, disagreement within the church is not inherently bad. Paul and Silas had a very big disagreement. The outcome of that disagreement actually strengthened the church and created new opportunities for both men and those who ministered with them. Again, the purpose of this book is not to determine which group or denomination is right or wrong in their theology, teaching, or mode of baptism. The purpose of this book is to ask why none of these groups are growing and then try to offer opportunities to change that.

There is however another group of churches not mentioned above. They are commonly referred to as nondenominational. These churches don't usually use that term as a heading in their name, but rather as a footnote. Their claim is that they are a self-sufficient group of like-minded individuals who control their own beliefs, teachings, and future with no ties to any national or international group. They live or die as a local church based on their own actions and support. Many of these churches, however, do have informal ties to other nondenominational churches. In fact, one of the goals of many of these churches is to start other independent nondenominational churches. I often wonder how many churches can be started by another nondenominational church before they actually do have a mini-denomination. I have often wondered at what point does your non-conformity make you a conformist?

In an article by Jay Guin posted on December 18, 2007 on the *One In Jesus* website he sites a book called *Beyond Megachurch Myths* that states that the U.S. grew by one-hundred million from the 1960s to 2006.[11] During that period while Hindu, Muslim and other religions have grown significantly the Christian Church attendance has remained constant over that forty year period. The authors point out that the megachurch movement is extraordinarily healthy. The number of megachurches, per one million people, has grown from

0.24 in 1970 to 4.00 in 2005, representing unbroken growth during this period. Of course, the total population has grown about 50% in this time, making the statistic all the more remarkable.

There is one unavoidable fact that separates denominational and nondenominational churches; the latter is growing and the former is not. Why? That actually gets to the core of my answer to the young lady who asked me about the resistance to change in our local church. My answer to her was *baggage.* In fact, it goes beyond baggage. It is as if denominational churches have rented storage facilities all across America and have filled them with baggage to the point where the thin metal security doors are bulging, ready to burst. In most cases, denominations have noticed the bulging doors and quickly responded by renting more space.

Most, if not all, nondenominational churches start from scratch. Most are born out of a few folks' frustration with the organized church and its failure to minister to the world. Very few of these churches start up because they just want a different style of music. At their base is a fundamental desire to minister to the community and to the world, to introduce others to Christ without the maintenance factor, or as stated earlier, the stressful need to just do what it takes to keep the doors open. Many of these churches start with no building or regular place to meet. There is no carpet to choose, no stained glass windows given in memory of a past member, no special hymnal, no organ purchased with funds from a ten year fundraising campaign, no Wednesday night Bible study, no set order of worship, no permanently installed furniture that prevents the use of other instruments and activity, no barriers to the use of modern technology like computers and LCD screens, and in most cases no long-term programs or folks who have been in charge of them for decades. In short, all of that stuff is baggage. Everything is new, and nothing is set in stone except the Word of God, like in Acts 2. Why don't you stop reading the book for a bit, pull out your Bible and turn to the second chapter of Acts. This would be a great time to review how church is supposed to operate.

This, the existence of baggage and how we handle it, in my

opinion, is the major difference between denominational and nondenominational churches. It is also the key to fixing this problem. It is important to note that denominational churches do not need to mirror nondenominational churches. What they must do, however, is dump the baggage mentioned above and develop their own unique ministry in their own community based on their own passion, gifts, and abilities. What the reconstruction looks like should be different for every congregation. Denominations need to allow more flexibility to local churches to allow them to develop ministries that are unique to their communities and spend less time concerned about preserving decades of kingdom building. That is where denominationalism tends to get in the way. Denominations have a tendency to do the work of the local church and regulate invention and Spirit-led direction. As I mentioned earlier, some denominations do this with casual pressure on their pastors. In my research, I have taken away two very important pieces of information from two of the most successful pastors in the nondenominational movement. I will leave them nameless because what they said is more important than who they are. I am sure that they would agree.

One of the pastors, when asked about why so many people attended his church, replied: "If you preach from God's word, without apology, your ministry will be blessed." The second pastor said, "It is important that you not copy what we have done. Be your own church; develop your identity in the community, and develop your own mission statement. The *way* we did it will not work for you, however, the *reason* we did will."

So, do you have to look like one of those mega-churches? Should you use their structure, brochures, literature, methods, music style, and so on? Absolutely not. What should you do? What should your church look like? Is your church unique? All of these questions and many more should be on your mind as you seek God's guidance through the Holy Spirit in breaking out of your mold. Don't be misled. If you have just begun this journey, prepare for a long trip. We are talking years. You might find yourself passing by the same intersection many times, as Moses did, while on your way to wherever you think you are being led. With what is at stake, however, it is worth the time and the effort. It may take generations if you have enough fuel left in your church. The sign post up ahead doesn't say abandon your denomination; it says change the structure, flip the model, get out of the box, but more importantly, get out of the church building, and start ministering to your community and to the world. Unlike when you travel on an airline, try to lose your baggage on this journey!

Five

Organized Boxes

What does it mean to get outside of the box? Does it mean to start doing things in such a dramatically different way that no one understands what's going on or, more importantly, what you are trying to say? It should not, but many times those who attempt to change their church's direction find themselves doing just that and merely add to the confusion. Being outside the box simply implies doing something in a meaningful, productive way that achieves a result that was not being achieved through traditional methods. That is *exactly* what Christ did.

Christ was outside the box. Was He a radical? I don't think so. He worked within the organized church to accomplish His purpose. That doesn't mean that He agreed with what they were doing. He also took action and spoke out vigorously against church policy and corruption. He even took apart their money enterprise at the temple in a violent rage. He did not however stand on the outside of the organization and throw stones through the windows. He did not say that the church, as they knew it then, was wrong; in fact, he taught from within it. What He taught was that they had corrupted the Law and that He did not come to destroy it, but to fulfill it. He redirected the church. Jim Henderson's book *a.k.a. Lost: Discovering Ways to Connect with the People Jesus Misses Most*, tells us that Christ had one hundred thirty-two encounters with people in the gospels.

Six were in the temple, four were in the synagogue, and one hundred twenty-two were in the daily course of life. We know there was more interaction with people than what is recorded in scripture; however, we have no reason to doubt that the percentages would be much the same if we could know all of those encounters.

Until this time, priests expected the people to come to them. Christ redefined the church. The early, organized church in the Old Testament had taken ten simple commandments, thrown in all of the details in Leviticus and Deuteronomy, and turned them into thousands of rules and procedures. Many of these man-made addendums provided the organized church the ability to profit from the people they were appointed to serve. Christ was clear in His teaching that God's commandments were not suggestions. However, He also pointed out that they were not black and white. He taught that the scriptures say thou shall not kill, but Christ went on to say that killing a person's reputation is just as sinful. Matthew 5:21-22, "You're familiar with the command to the ancients, 'Do not murder.' I'm telling you that anyone who is so much as angry with a brother or sister is guilty of murder. Carelessly call a brother 'idiot!' and you just might find yourself hauled into court. Thoughtlessly yell 'stupid!' at a sister and you are on the brink of hellfire. The simple moral fact is that words kill."

Christ ministered, not only outside the walls of the church, but also to otherwise neglected groups of people. He ministered to women who were considered property, not worthy of such instruction. He ministered to Gentiles, drunks, whores, the poor, the rich, church leaders, Roman soldiers and certainly to children whom He compared to heaven itself. He was everything the organized church was not. Was this outside the box? Yes. Was it understandable to the people to whom He was ministering? Yes. Was it effective? Over two thousand years of Christianity, even with it's warts, would say yes it was and is.

Blended Worship Services

I have had several pastors and music ministers call me and ask what I thought of blended worship, which is using several styles of music and worship formats in one service? Well, we tried it about ten years ago. It seemed like a good idea at the time, a chance to give everyone what they wanted. You know that kind of lukewarm, fuzzy feeling. Having grown up in the 1960s pleasing everyone sounded like a practical solution to me. The results were tragic.

To understand why blended worship did not work, one must look more closely at church *family* relationships. Not the relatives that are in the church, but the spiritual family, or so it is called. On the surface, most churches boast that they are a family. Everyone wants to help and understand and be the *Partridge Family*. There are very few, if any, families in existence that act the way most churches think they are structured. There are three aspects of the family metaphor as it relates to the church. First is the family reunion mentality, the attitude that we take care of our own. That should be the comforting side of belonging to a family. Second, there is the less pleasant aspect of the family, the one where nobody likes Uncle Charlie for who knows what reason, other than that he is just not a likeable guy, and everyone talks about him behind his back. Finally, there is the third side of family that no one seems to understand when related to church—the outsider. For instance, what family would allow a total stranger to have complete access to their house after meeting them just once? Probably no one in their right mind would do that. Furthermore, if the church will turn on someone already in the family, what will it do to someone who is invited into the family who, without being asked, decides to make a suggestion or change something that has been done within that family the same way for decades? When viewed from this angle, family is probably not a good term to use to describe bringing others to the Body of Christ.

Blended worship was one such family matter in our church. We, the elders, talked to both sides and had what we thought was a mutual understanding of the issue. The result was that those who wanted change were willing to give and take, and those who wanted no change were the Rock of Gibraltar.

When you think about it, even the term "blended" sounds like a disaster. Have you ever looked at or drunk a blended mixture of vegetables? They say it is good for you, but for the most part you can't tell what is in it, and it tastes like the color gray. Blended is not out of the box. Rather, it is the same thing in the box with the top off and maybe turned in a different direction. In the end, it is the same box. It is an effort to please too many people and in so doing, actually confuses the issue of what should be changed or modified to revitalize growth.

Unfortunately, the very word "change" suggests stress and pain. For change to take place, something has to be displaced and reshaped into something totally different. Such a feat can be very traumatic within a family. It can be done, however, in a body of believers who are modeling their efforts after the very inventor of change—Christ.

When looking at your church, you must take an honest look at everything, even those programs or activities that are considered successful. None of this should be done, however, until you have first determined God's direction. That is going to take a while. In the next few chapters, my ministry partners and I will give you some guidelines on how to accomplish that very important first step. Before reading any further I invite you to start examining the inside of your box.

Six

Why Do Churches Fail?

Some Churches May Need to Die in Order to Be Reborn

I have attended several sales schools in my career. One phrase I have heard over and over is, "Most people do not plan to fail; they just fail to plan." I think that is a good explanation of what is going on in most failing churches today. No one stood up in a meeting and said, "I make a motion that we intentionally try to get our attendance to decline and we stop ministering to our community." Like many of you, I have heard some silly motions, but never one to intentionally kill the church. This problem arose over a long period of time from the assumption that things would always be the way they are.

Many of us live our lives believing that tomorrow will be pretty much like today. We think that the friends we have will always be our friends. We think that the job we have will always be our job. Parents think that they will always have children in their house (and some do). We go to bed every night thinking that we will wake up in the same land of freedom.

Sometimes, our world is shattered because things beyond our control change our lives in the blink of an eye. Some of these are personal, friends move away; businesses downsize, causing jobs to be lost; children graduate from high school and move out. Others are not ordinary and affect the entire world, like two passenger jets flying into the World Trade Center. In the real world, things change every day. Sometimes I wonder if the church is in the real world because it seems to be unaffected by life outside its stained glass walls. For some, the church is a snapshot in time, a place of refuge from everything else that changes. Sometimes the only way to stop that endless cycle of denial is for there to be a death. Sometimes a church or a denomination just needs to die.

Yes, that is a dramatic statement; however, it is not an unreasonable statement. Let's begin with Christ. Christ had to die to be resurrected. Why? He had to bury all of our sin that occupied the world then and now. He could not fix it. There had to be a sacrifice. Jesus clearly pointed out the sins of the world and of the organized church. When He died, all of that was drawn into His death and eliminated forever, including the veil of the temple that separated us from God. Just think about the Jewish people who had for centuries relied on a priest to be their spokesperson and a place called the "Holiest of Holies" that sat behind a curtain that was, in an instant, changed. Think about what a drastic change that was for those people. Now consider how different from the temple of Jesus' day is a church that digs in its heels and refuses to change?

Next let's talk about the following passage in 2 Corinthians 5:17: "Now we look inside, and what we see is that anyone united with the Messiah gets a fresh start, is created new. The old life is gone; a new life burgeons! Look at it! All this comes from the God who settled the relationship between us and him, and then called us to settle our relationships with each other." This is one of Paul's most personal letters. He, more than anyone, came from a life that surely seemed as if it would never change. Before his conversion, he went to bed hating Christians and awoke with the same urgency to stop them at any cost. God went so far as to remove one of Paul's most relied upon learning tools, his eyesight. Ironically, only then could Paul *see* that his world had to change. That event had to be in the back of his memory when he penned the words in this passage. For him, old things were truly passed away. They had died! What rose from those ruins was a wonderful, powerful new life. What if God had tried to change Paul just a little bit? What if God had tried to *blend* him in? Why should the church (the organization) be exempt from the same conversion process as those who are part of the church, the people?

Again, sometimes the only hope for a church is that it be allowed to die. But, just like Christ, though the church dies, the people do not. The people are wonderfully reborn and resurrected from the ashes! Some will become active in other churches; some may bind together in a new spirit and start another church without any baggage. Others, those who may have been so committed to the old ministry, may finally understand what the church should be, or maybe they will just be attracted to some other dying church. In the end, it is not the church building that provides the ministry or ministry opportunities. It is God working through people. Christ can resurrect His work, but first He may need to get the church building and all that has become attached to it over the decades out of the way.

Communities' Change

In a meeting recently, our pastor asked the elders to raise their hands if they at one time lived in or near the zip code of our church. Most raised their hands. Then he asked how many still live in proximity of the church. Less than 20 percent raised their hands. Our church as a whole reflects that same percentage. What happened?

My home church, the Tusculum Church, celebrated its one hundred fiftieth birthday a while back. Most of those one hundred fifty years were on a piece of property down the road from our current location. In 1986, God directed us to exchange churches with a dying, ironically, independent non-denominational Baptist church. You see, this was a nondenominational church because it had no affiliation with any other Baptist churches. Not all nondenominational churches make it, but this one did revive after we exchanged properties and, once it had time to reevaluate its purpose and make positive changes. The exchange allowed the church to regain its momentum and recover to do what it was called to do, ministering to its community in its own unique way. Its parking lot is full again. In reality, the Baptist church died. There were dramatic changes in that church. They had been a very large congregation that ran a school system including kindergarten through high school. When we exchanged facilities, there were about four families left trying to support and maintain a huge physical plant. Unlike the Baptist church that vacated our new property, I am not sure that our church had the same experience.

We took over a much larger facility than the one we exchanged with the independent Baptist congregation. After a few years, we built on to that facility. We did show early growth in our congregation, however, events were on the horizon that would stop that growth and place us in a position similar to that of the previous occupants. In addition to internal changes, our community was changing before our eyes, mostly in respect to economics, ethnicity, and age distribution. While we did not spend much time formally discussing the changing community and how it might effect our church, some expressed concerns about the situation privately.

Like many communities in America, the area around our church had a large increase in Central American and Asian people over about a ten year period. Prior to that our community was a mix of mostly black and white, but this new mix was unsettling to most. There were plenty of segregated black and white congregations, and now several of the smaller, vacated church buildings left by congregations that had moved or disbanded were converted to Spanish-speaking churches. Business signs along the major road were now either in Spanish and English or Spanish alone. Used car lots and Mexican businesses were appearing at a maddening pace. Everything around our congregation was changing. Where there had been two dominate cultures, now there were four.

The community surrounding our church was very well established, and many of the homes were built in the late fifties and early sixties. Those who had purchased the homes had most likely finished paying off their thirty-year mortgages and were, of course, growing older. Many of these owners were retired or disabled. The homes of the elderly who were passing away or moving into assisted living homes were being bought up by young, first-time buyers. As with all urban development, undeveloped land was bought up, and apartment buildings began to appear. In other words the economy of the area was declining and along with it the ministry needs of the community that our church should have been preparing to address.

Four well established community churches in our area sold their facilities, moved out of the community, and built new campuses. Two of the churches were sold to Spanish-speaking congregations; a third was sold to a Coptic Church, and the fourth, as of this writing, has yet to be sold.

So what were we doing during all of those years of change? For the past seventeen years, we have produced a very successful passion play for our community. The passion play is a drama about the last days of Christ's life on earth. It has attracted thousands of people of all faiths and ethnic backgrounds. We have testimony from many who attended over the years that sent us letters telling us that the presentation changed their lives. During this period, we also have sponsored a peewee basketball program for the community involving between one hundred and one hundred fifty five, six, and seven-year olds. Many of these children are underprivileged. This program has also succeeded in reaching people in our community and changing lives. Our youth ministry brings in over sixty youth on any given Wednesday evening for their Bible study (compared to an average of two hundred fifty attendees of all ages on Sunday mornings). Youth of all backgrounds have been introduced to Christ through the Bible study. The church body however, the people, were dying, in some cases literally. Our older members were dying or moving into nursing facilities. Others were discouraged by changes that were suggested by leadership and moved to other churches. Some wanted change to happen more quickly and simply found another church, and some members where moving to new neighborhoods as they climbed the economic ladder or sought what they perceived to be better school districts.

As a result, our church began to decline as we continued to focus on, and pat ourselves on the back for, the few good things we were doing. We also set our sights on trying to pay off a mortgage. We did not plan to fail; we just failed to plan for these changes and adjust. It appeared that suddenly everything had changed but us. In reality, it had been changing for years, and perhaps we chose to ignore it.

No Outreach

I have a friend who reminds me that churches need to have *up-reach, in-reach,* and *outreach.* He is absolutely correct. Without a balance of these three things, the church body cannot have a holistic ministry. Two of these are easy for most churches. *Up-reach* is a connection to God, a longing for His presence in our lives. Without that, there is no church. The Lord knows we know how to do *in-reach.* We are masters at taking care of ourselves. *Outreach,* however, is not just lacking in most churches, but often completely misunderstood.

Outreach is often labeled as *missions* or *missionary work,* overseas of course. If you look at most churches' foundational structure, you will find that the organization is built on a foundation of worship, primarily the Sunday morning experience. It is no wonder that churches come apart when someone messes with that piece of the foundation. Try messing with their missions program, and see how much trouble you start. All you will get is a blank stare because most folks will not know what you are talking about, or they are happy to allow you to do anything you like. After all, you will be doing all the work, so what is it to them?

Just so we are all talking about the same thing, let's define outreach for the purpose of this discussion. Outreach includes missions, but it also consists of a thousand other subtle things that bind a body of believers to the very heart of God. Outreach could be defined as God using us to reach those who need to be reached. Has your church specifically defined who that might be? Do you have a specific plan to accomplish that goal? Do you have a way of measuring that result? Do you have a way of training people to accomplish that goal, or is your vision as vague as, "We just want to win the lost to Christ?" While that last statement sounds real churchy and religious, it is actually the testimony of a non-growth church's inability to do what they say they want to do. Please read this last paragraph a couple of more times. It is important that you agree or disagree. It will determine how you except or reject the remainder of this book.

If you want to change your community for Christ, you must flip your foundational model upside down and place outreach as the primary building block while making the worship service the smallest component. I will address this later in more detail.

No Training

When our church finally started looking at our problem, it became evident that intentional, specifically tailored training was almost nonexistent. Training in our church was restricted to sermons, Sunday school, Wednesday night Bible study, and our youth program. Most deeply religious matters were confined to the pastor. Additionally, there were no expectations for people to have *any* training before they were thrust into positions of leadership.

Most congregations hire staff to do the work of the church. Growing churches hire staff to *train* others to do the work of the church. How can so many churches overlook such a simple concept? I call it lazy laity. OK, if you are not clergy, now *you* hate me. I can live with that. If you finish the book, you may forgive me.

Some blame, though not the greater part, can be placed at the feet of the pastor. That is because the pastor allows it to happen. Many pastors allow their congregations to dump most of the responsibility at their feet. In some cases, pastors want the responsibility for job security. Regardless of the reason, it is wrong. Everyone in your church that could be considered staff, whether paid or volunteer, has a responsibility to replace themselves. That includes the pastor. When these folks die or move on, they should leave a legacy, not an empty desk or office. That is their responsibility. On the other hand, what is the responsibility of the laity? Establishing expectations.

There should be an expectation on the part of the congregation that staff will identify and train leaders. There should be expectation of the laity to get involved and find resources that will help them train themselves. This is how a culture of learning is established and promoted within a church. This will require a lot more change than adding praise songs and a drummer to a worship service.

No Evangelism

Evangelism is the act of bringing others to Christ just as Andrew brought Peter. It wasn't that Peter had never heard of Jesus. On the contrary, he had heard him and His message. Peter, however, had never had a personal relationship with Him. That is where Andrew came in. Andrew brought Peter into direct contact with Jesus. When he did, Jesus spoke to Peter's heart. That is the important part of evangelism and the primary reason we should have it in our body of believers. There is, however, another side to evangelism. Evangelism is the very act of replacing ourselves in the work of God.

There was an interesting sect of people called the Shakers (the United Society of Believers) founded by Ann Lee in 1772. The group splintered from the Quakers because of the Shakers unusual theological beliefs and their mode of worship. The group was known for their celibacy, which obviously led to their demise. If you cannot replace yourself, whatever you are doing will soon come an end. If a church is not bringing others to a personal relationship with Christ and then providing an avenue to ministry and spiritual maturity, the church will be short-lived. This is exactly what is happening to churches across America.

One of the saddest meetings I have ever attended was a biannual meeting of the Nashville Presbytery of the Cumberland Presbyterian Denomination. During those meetings, about thirty-eight churches reported on their congregations. One church's name was called, and an elderly man slowly walked to the front of the church. When he turned, you could see tears in his eyes. His voice was shaking as he informed the group that one of their longtime members had recently passed away. He was sad at the loss of his longtime friend, but he was even more saddened that he had to report to presbytery that there were now only three members left in their church. Most of them, he said, would not make it through the next year. He ended by saying, "I guess we will just have to close the church."

Did that church completely fail to evangelize? No, there were records of people being saved and joining that fellowship. The church had been around for many, many years. Although there were certainly other reasons that contributed to the demise of this church, failure of the members to use evangelism to replace themselves surely was a major contributor. Again, if we are following Christ's commandment, how can this happen? There are churches closing their doors every day in America. Just drive around your town. They are there; you have to look for them. That is the problem; people have always had to look for them.

Refusal to Change

I have touched on this several times already, but I list it here because it is a major reason that churches die. The sad part is that many churches are in disarray over changes that are the least important part of their organization. You could infer that I am saying that worship is not important, but let me quickly say that everything a church does is important. Let me make the statement again:

"The sad part is that many churches are in disarray over changes that are the *least* important part of their organization."

I mentioned earlier that the foundational structure of most churches makes the worship service the pivotal part of their ministry. Because of that emphasis, the worship service seems to be the obvious place to make changes. If you make the other *hard* changes, like getting your structural priorities right, first, worship will take care of itself. If the size of your church doubles, there will likely be a demand for a different emphasis in worship from the new people who then attend.

Churches used to split over theological issues. Today, sadly, most folks who attend church don't know enough about the theology of their church to become upset. We really are building our houses on sand.

Too Much Debt

A few years ago, at an elders' retreat, our leadership made a pledge to take the steps needed to reverse our decline and start accomplishing God's purpose in our fellowship. Part of that pledge centered on our obligation to stewardship. Our leadership adopted the following pledge and we have held to it ever since. Although we did not reach our goal set for January 1, 2006, we did reduce our indebtedness by over $250,000 in a very short period of time. We are now under $400,000 and we can see victory over this issue in our future. We realized that much of the money we have put toward debt since 1998 can eventually be turned to ministry outside the walls once the debt is paid. Probably the most important part of the pledge was in the second paragraph. We have not altered from that pledge once and have no intentions of doing so, although a recent roof problem tested our resolve and our faith.

Please read the following motion of our session made at the previously mentioned retreat.

A Pledge to Keep

We, the Session of the Tusculum Cumberland Presbyterian Church, hereby pledge, acknowledging first our belief that God is the creator of everything, that we will collectively and individually do everything within our ability to pay off our existing indebtedness, without sacrificing any current, ongoing ministries, by January 1, 2006.

We further pledge that from this day forward we will, and we encourage our congregation, to rely only on the promise of God that He will supply all our needs. Therefore, the Tusculum Church will become a debt free church and from this day forward will not borrow money from any source but rely on the stewardship and generosity of our congregation as they feel led to give back to God a portion of that which He has so richly blessed.

After years of ignoring stained, drooping ceiling tiles, a major roof leak presented itself in a main hallway next to the fellowship hall. A major rain storm caused a flood in that part of the building and it became clear that we needed to fix the roof, not patch it. After receiving several bids, the church leaders determined that it would take about $125,000 to complete the project. We had about $15,000 in the "rainy day fund."

We had known for years that this day was coming. We knew that we should have been setting money aside. Instead the church continued to try to pay off the debt, even with declining attendance and income. In fact, the church had several special offerings to reduce our debt that brought in significant funds. In short, the church was just maintaining. Now we had a $125,000 problem that could not be ignored, $15,000 in the bank, and a pledge that had been made to God and the church not to borrow money.

What happened next is testimony to the spiritual growth that has occurred in our congregation, most notably our leadership, in the last two years. The elders met, discussed the problem, and outlined the options, all of which seemed unacceptable or unattainable. Those options were to do nothing, to fix the roof by borrowing the money, thus breaking the pledge, or to go to the congregation and pray that God would take charge. Leadership wisely chose the third option while at the same time securing assurance from the bank that we could borrow the funds if needed. Setting up the line of credit was the church's way of saying, *maybe* God can do this, but maybe He has other plans. Although the leadership had grown considerably, there was still a way to go before they completely understood God's challenge to test Him as outlined in Malachi 3:8-10. "Begin by being honest. Do honest people rob God? But you rob me day after day." You ask, 'How have we robbed you?' "The tithe and the offering—that's how! And now you're under a curse, the whole lot of you, because you're robbing me. Bring your full tithe to the Temple treasury so there will be ample provisions in my Temple. Test me in this and see if I don't open up heaven itself to you and pour out blessings beyond your wildest dreams."

As you will see, God proved His point. That too, was a growing experience.

Those in charge of the project explained the need to the church body and reminded the congregation of the pledge that was previously made. Everyone was encouraged to pray about the need. The end result was that after six months, over $140,000 had been raised! A lot of folks grew in several areas of their Christian journey through this experience, learning to rely fully on God's promise and how to give expecting nothing in return. There were two very interesting issues entwined in this ordeal. First, during the extended period that we were raising the funds, the area was experiencing a drought of historic proportions. Did God punish farmers and others who desperately needed the rain? No. However, He did use a bad situation to bless our congregation while we gathered in the donations He provided. No further damage was done to our facility while we raised the money.

The second issue is even more dramatic and important. When it became apparent that the roof could no longer be ignored, our church was in the middle of a realization that to grow out of our maintenance mode, we needed to hire an additional staff member — a young adult pastor. No sooner had the church made the decision to do something positive to grow, then circumstances seemed to set back those efforts for years to come. What actually happened was that the leadership and the church, through this adversity, grew to understand that they could sacrifice, that they could afford to hire an additional staff person. God works in ways we will never understand. He had to create an opportunity for us to choose to believe in Him and ourselves. God is good!

There is a popular movie about a man who had a dream of building a baseball park on his farm. He meets a gentleman who tells him, "If you build it, they will come." Unfortunately, like the movie, many churches think this means that if they build facilities, people will come and fill them up. It would be more accurate to say, "If you build it, it will sit." Further, "If you build it with borrowed money, it will sit while the loan is a millstone on your ministry for years."

Debt is a way of life for most Americans. That naturally carries over into our church experience. Our nation has rightly been characterized as a *microwave society*. We want it, and we want it now! We should be able to enjoy things while we pay for them. There are many opinions about this matter within the church. There are good arguments on both sides of the issue. The simple matter, however, is that if you go into debt for facilities, you will pay more than if you pay upfront due to the added interest. It is also true that debt will become a primary focus of many conservatives in the church, and they will likely ignore important ministry opportunities just to pay off debt. This is a recipe for disagreement within the church. It is also very difficult to teach sacrifice to your congregation if the church doesn't practice it. If you closely observe a church that is declining, you might find debt at its core. If it is so, it may not be possible to reverse the direction without a miracle. You might ignore the Lord for a while, but you will always answer the phone when the bank calls.

Failure to Recognize and Structure Generational Bridges

If Satan ever had a natural weapon to use on the Christian church, age gaps have to be it. For over a hundred years, church leaders attempted to minister to the church as a whole. For the most part, they were somewhat successful. There was one method to reach anyone who walked through the door. Furthermore, when the church did get out in the streets, there was only one approach, regardless of the age of the target. Many times that is exactly what people were, targets.

Generational bridges are simply methods of ministering to one age group in a way that allows them to naturally move through the life of the church without creating gaps of spiritual growth, caused by a failure to provide relevant teaching and ministry opportunities. There will be several opportunities to use these bridges throughout the life of the person and the church.

In the late fifties and sixties, the church, along with many secular interests, started to realize that there are two distinct age groups, young and old. Marketing methods changed and, to a lesser degree, the church started to appeal to the newfound "younger generation." The dividing line was somewhere between college and adulthood, whatever that meant.

As time marched on, society began to change more quickly, and these two groups divided again. On the adult side, people were living longer, even retiring from their first occupations and starting entirely new careers. On the younger side, a widening gap developed between the maturity level of high school and college students.

Then in the nineties, things started to get complicated. Noticeable gaps began to appear between the *builders*, the group who survived World War II and built the structure of modern America, and the *boomers*, a very large group of people who were born beginning right after the end of World War II. In addition, there was a third group born between 1965 and 1976 called the *busters* . Later divisions would complicate this even further.

There were also significant divisions developing in the younger set. Today, the differences have become so refined that brothers and sisters fewer than three years apart have striking likes and dislikes in clothes, music, food, ethics, religion and politics. There seems to be no end to this continuous division of our society in America. A great book to read on this subject is *One Church, Four Generations* by Gary L. McIntosh.[12]

Think for a moment about trying to minister to such a diverse group in one church. Satan has to be smiling from ear to ear. Society has placed an almost impossible barricade to ministry in the modern church with these divisions. At the heart of many dying churches, this problem has either been ignored, or more likely, deemed unfixable. For many churches, this one problem can prevent them from ever becoming the church they could be. This is one opportunity that a church will either work its way through with God's help or simply give up.

Good news laymen, there are thousands of churches who have worked through this situation and stomped all over Satan's smiling face! How did they do it? They simply stopped looking at it as a problem and went to work educating themselves about the different groups. They most likely found that there were several of these groups within their own church, regardless of how small the congregation was. The success was most likely in addressing the issue not ignoring it.

Power

Most pastors will acknowledge that there are a few people within their congregations who hold power over many decisions made in the church. Their positions stem from various sources: money, time in the church, community position, educational background, personality, large family in the membership, etc. Some of these folks are very outspoken, and some are as cunning as a stealth fighter jet pilot. The latter group is the one that makes my blood pressure skyrocket.

There is a difference between power and opinion. An opinion is not inherently wrong; it is how you choose to advocate that opinion that decides its fate. You might even have an agenda, and that is also not wrong if properly applied. But, if you abuse your position within the church, you should be excommunicated and sent to live with what may be left of the Shakers. You definitely should not be allowed to reproduce. No one said this was easy.

I overheard someone in our church say that if the leadership did not return to the way we had been doing things, they would withhold their money. Basically, they were blackmailing God. I realized that this was actually a failure of our church to educate folks about stewardship. It is one of those overlooked issues that a once-a-year sermon will not correct.

I once had an hour long discussion with a gentleman over the phrase, "We give to God for the work of the church." He insisted that it read, "We give to the church for the work of God." Why? Because he wanted the right to have a say in what the church did with his money! If he was giving it to God, that short-circuited his control.

I heard of a church in Northern Tennessee that had a large argument over the color of roofing tiles that were going to be placed on the church. There were two large contributors, and both felt that they should have the right to choose the color. A well-meaning pastor intervened and suggested that they put one color on one side and the other color on the other side. That way, each could sit under the color he chose. Don't you know that decision unified the church? Probably not.

Christ was not careless with His use of words. Often we misuse the words *every time, always, all,* and *never.* Note His use of the word *all* in the following verse: "Then Jesus came to them and said, "*All* authority in heaven and on earth has been given to me." (Matthew 28:18 NIV). He gave none of it to us! It is also important to note that this is almost the last thing He said before being caught up into Heaven. It is equally interesting that the last order He gave was to get out of the church building. Actually, He said, "Jesus, undeterred, went right ahead and gave his charge: God authorized and commanded me to commission you: *Go out* and train everyone you meet, far and near, in this way of life, marking them by baptism in the threefold name: Father, Son, and Holy Spirit. Then instruct them in the practice of all I have commanded you. I'll be with you as you do this, day after day after day, right up to the end of the age" (Matthew 28:18—20 the Message).

In these three verses, Jesus addresses all the reasons churches fail that I listed in this chapter. Here is a short summary of those root causes. *Some churches may need to die in order to be reborn.* Starting over can be healthy. *Communities change.* Failure to plan for inevitable change will make it almost impossible to recover once a church realizes the problem. *No outreach.* A church needs upreach, in-reach, and out-reach. Just having two out of three is bad. *No training.* Expecting the pastor to be the only spiritual mentor is overwhelming and robs the congregation of beautiful ministry opportunities. *No evangelism.* The church needs to have a missions focused ministry that goes into the community and draws people to Christ. *Refusal to change.* Realizing that Christ was the definition of change within the church is the first step toward effective ministry. *Too much debt.* God said to bring *all* the tithes into the storehouse and *test Me* to see if I will not pour out on you a blessing you cannot contain. *Generational Bridges.* Overcoming Satan's natural weapon of age gaps can empower a congregation to build for the future by utilizing untapped resources within the Body of Christ by uniting rather than dividing. *Power.* Those within the church fight an eternal battle similar to the one staged by Satan when he attempted to ascend to the very throne of God.

The first step to solving any problem is admitting that you have one. I have often wondered if there should be a "churches anonymous" support group where laymen and clergy could meet once a week. Each one would get up in front of the group and begin their address by saying, "Hello, my name is John Smith. I am a non-conformist conformist church member who can't stand change for any possible reason. I have been clean for thirteen weeks." And the group says, "Hello John, we love you."

Maybe our prayer should be, "Father, forgive us for overlooking the simple stuff."

Seven

The Sequoia Lesson

I have referred to my home church on several occasions throughout this book. Before I tell you some marvelous results from our church's struggle with change, I want to summarize my thoughts using the largest living thing in the world, the giant sequoia.

In my day job, I often have to drive for many hours to get to a client's location. Those journeys often take me through rural communities, forests, and farmland. I am always intrigued by a single tree that stands out from everything around it. There is something unique about the tree's shape, color, size, and even the way the light hits it. On a trip to Yosemite National Park, I encountered several trees that demanded my undivided attention—the giant sequoias.

Frank, our guide, mentioned several interesting things that caused me to think about the focus of this book and the relationship between these awesome trees and our Christian growth. I picked up a small book at the gift shop, *the Sequoias of Yosemite National Park*, by H. Thomas Harvey,[13] and was amazed that many of the growth patterns and attributes of this tree mirror our Christian journey, both good and bad.

First, I was in awe as I stood before the "Grizzly Giant," a tree that stands in the Mariposa Grove at the Southern entrance to Yosemite Park, realizing that it began its life about five hundred to eight hundred years *before* Jesus was born. The tree is still very much alive, with some branches measuring six feet in diameter! The tree is a little over two hundred feet tall and is over thirty-one feet in diameter at the base.

The Grizzly Giant is a mature sequoia and has been for centuries. It has endured floods, fires, wind, heavy snows, other falling trees, lightening, pollution, and old age. Yet its roots, reaching out some one hundred fifty feet in all directions, are only two to three feet below the surface. Although I am nowhere near the size of this living monument, while looking at the tree, I saw a model of my Christian life standing right in front of me.

I have grown in my faith, and I try to live my life each day so that others will notice, not me, but Jesus. However, as strong as my faith may be, my roots are also right below the surface. I became curious about how something as large as this tree could continue to stand through centuries of adversity with such shallow roots. The answer, as expected, was in the roots. It gave me a new perspective about my Christian growth and how dependent that growth is on those who surround me.

Roots

The roots of a giant sequoia start out much like any tree. There is a tap root that grows straight down looking for moisture and nourishment. At the same time, other roots begin to grow out from the tree. That process continues for six to eight years. After that, the tap root actually stops growing and dies. In this process, the lateral roots, which grow straight out from the base, increase their growth, eventually stretching up to four acres in a mature tree.

The sequoia root growth pattern should be a picture of our own Christian growth. When someone accepts Christ, they should bury themselves in the word, digging straight down into God's directions for their life. It is important that new Christians surround themselves with mature Christians who can supply moisture (knowledge) and nourishment (Christian example) for their life. After a period of time boring our *tap root* deep into a new life in Christ, attention should shift to our lateral roots. Unlike the giant sequoia, our tap root does not die but is eternally connected to the source of all growth, God Himself. These small lateral roots should not be deep in the ground where the world is blocked from view and kept from affecting our lives. The roots should be deep enough to keep us anchored, but shallow enough for us to occasionally poke through the ground, exposing who we are and allowing the world to come into contact with us and us with them.

This contact, as it relates to the church, hits right at the heart of our modern small church death spiral. A church is not a bomb shelter; it is a hospital open to everyone who is seeking a change. That is the internal, often unspoken conflict within the church. Most lay people within a dying church just do not talk about this issue. It is understood that since they are doing all of the traditional church stuff, there must be some other undiscoverable reason for the decline of their church.

If someone comes into a church looking for a change in their life, and all they see is no change, what are they to think? Outsiders who come into your church should see a living, growing organism that is constantly molding itself to fit the needs of those who are coming through the doors but not changing the message of Jesus' love for us or what he did for us. People who are looking for solutions to their problems cannot find it by molding themselves to your unchanging agenda. Unfortunately, failure to be available and adapt to the needs of a hurting world is only half the problem. The other half involves never developing a tap root at all, but just running weak, ineffective roots across the lawn to give the appearance of a caring church. There is a television advertisement for a car that expresses this well. They use the term *social camouflage*. What a perfect description of our world.

Many churches attempt to adopt the successful methods of growing churches without developing deep spiritual roots of their own. Developing deep roots is not an easy process, nor can it be accomplished quickly. It will not happen by accident, but it can begin just as naturally as the growth pattern of the sequoia if we allow the same God who grows those trees to guide us.

There was still something missing in the physics of the sequoia root system that made me wonder what kept these giants from tipping over in a good wind after a heavy snow melt. To put this in perspective, if you were to lay one of these trees on its side in a football stadium, it would run from goal line to goal line, and its branches would reach a third of the way into the stands on both sides. I have seen large oak trees with deep roots lying on their sides with the roots sticking out after a heavy season of rain. These large sequoias sometimes endure as much as thirty feet of snow which then melts and settles into the soil. There are often fifty to sixty mile-per-hour winds that blow through the forest, yet these trees continue to stand and grow! How?

Again, the answer is in the root system. Much of the root system in a mature sequoia is thread-like. While some of the branches can be six feet in diameter, many of the roots are one foot or less in diameter. From these roots run thousands of small thread-like roots that weave complex patterns into the soil. The combined tensile roots are unbelievably strong, much like Velcro. These small threads also do a better job of collecting needed moisture and nourishment from their surroundings. Isn't that what a church should look like? If you compare a healthy church to one that is dying, you will find this contrast. In an effective church, you will find multiple small roots (the laymen using their God-given gifts and talents in God's calling). In a small or, for that matter, large, dying church, you will likely find only a few large roots that are trying to support the tree. The latter is a tree that is destined for failure and a place on the forest floor.

Fire

In recent years, the forestry service and firefighters in general have discovered the error of their ways in trying to prevent *all* forest fires. Nature knows best and regularly sets fires by lightening.

Conservationists have discovered that, by putting out fires, underbrush grows out of control, and falling limbs build up, providing an excellent fuel source for an out of control fire. By allowing forest fires to take their natural course, this underbrush is constantly cleared and future fires are much more controllable. In fact, the forest service now regularly sets fires.

Also, in recent years it was discovered that the sequoia cannot effectively reproduce without fire. Only through the heat of a fire can the seeds be broken out of their cells and deposited on the forest floor in a way that will allow growth.

As with our Christian life, the mighty sequoia must face adversity to grow and prevail over that adversity. We must not make a habit of removing obstacles from the path of those who are attempting to grow, for if we do, we also remove the opportunity for learning and growth. Just as strong winds teach a tree how to bend and not break in a storm, adversity teaches us how to deal with life and the world. Church should not be a danger-free zone. If, however, we never get out into the world as a church, that is exactly what it becomes.

If a Tree Falls in the Forest

The age-old question remains; if a tree falls in the forest and no one is there to hear it, will there be a noise? According to my high school science teacher, yes there would be a noise, that is, if you consider a vibration noise. Our absence from the forest does not remove the laws of physics or vibration. In addition, noise is defined as vibration, not our ears picking up the vibration.

How are your actions perceived in your church? Do people see and hear your ministry? More importantly, what will happen when you are gone, when you fall in the forest? Understanding what happens when a giant sequoia dies and falls in the grove might help illustrate the importance of planning for that inevitable event. The answer involves fertility and growth. The seeds of the giant trees are very small, about the same size of a single flake of dry oatmeal.

Under normal conditions, these seeds are blocked by foliage and never make it to the hard forest floor. When one of these mature trees fall, it not only makes a great noise; the ripped roots, yanked from the forest floor, loosen the soil for falling seeds. The falling tree also takes smaller brush down with it, clearing the way for sunlight that otherwise may never have reached the small seed.

It is so important that we leave a legacy in the wake of our journey through this life. When it is time for us to step aside, we should have properly prepared the soil where we have walked. Our walking around in our ministries should not pack down the ground beneath our feet. Instead, we should have a plow hooked up behind us that constantly turns over new soil. That cannot happen if we are not open to new things and…*change!* We should have taken the time to prepare someone to do what we do. Some of our life's journey should have been spent in teaching what we have learned. However, the Christian life is a process, not an assembly line. Remember the story Jesus told of the seeds falling on three different types of ground. This is certainly a vivid example of that parable.

Unimportant Effectiveness

There is one last thing about these magnificent trees I find interesting. As the tour bus rounded a curve, the driver stepped on the brake and slowed to a gentle stop. Before the tour bus driver spoke, it was obvious that something was very different. Most of the large front window was filled with an enormous burnt orange bark. The object dwarfed everything else in view. I loved the driver's comment, "This is one of the smaller trees." A sequoia sticks out in a crowd, not because it is more important than any of the other trees, but because it commands your eyes to look at it. When we did get to the "big" tree, I had the same feeling I had when I stood on the precipice of the Grand Canon. It was simply indescribable. The tree didn't ask me to think that it was more important than others, just different. Isn't that what Christ asks of us? Just as the large tree created awe without saying anything, our lives and individual ministries should have the same effect. An old saying comes to mind, "Preach a sermon everyday. Use words if necessary."

The great sequoia tree is a perfect introduction to a marvelous story of discovery, vision, and the change of a church that went beyond the norm—my church, the Tusculum Church. We are not through with this journey and may never be because what we have discovered is a vision, not a series of goals; opportunity, not maintenance; and connection to a community, not a provider of endless programs. It has become an exciting, marvelous trip. Not surprisingly we call it *Our Journey, Life on the Road to Eternity*. We will spend the rest of our time offering solutions instead of dwelling on problems. Please, come along and walk with me.

Eight

Our Journey: The Tusculum Story

Before beginning this chapter, I want to again give thanks to my home church for putting up with my annoying persistence regarding vision and expectations. They know where my heart lies and that my head must be in the same general vicinity. I have always believed that God was leading this discussion and that I was simply one of His vehicles at the time. I am not special, nor did God give me anything that cannot be acquired by someone else. Maybe I just listened. Listening to God is most often not a popular course of action. Perhaps God was attracted to my Teflon skin.

Thank you Tusculum Church, and forgive me if I got a few of the events out of order.

In previous chapters, I have outlined several of the ongoing problems faced by our church over the past few years. In short, Tusculum was a typical small church struggling to keep members, trying to make sensible changes, and wondering why nothing seemed to be working to improve growth. I will not reintroduce those specific problems, but rather spend more productive time talking about what the church chose to do. It is important to note that the Tusculum Church has not had adequate time to experience complete recovery or start to show significant growth. Such a process takes years, not months.

What we have seen, however, is God at work in unique ways in the individual lives of some of our folks. Scripture assures us that such evidence is a precursor of God's coming blessing. There could be no better example of this assurance for those who follow God's will than the wonderful account of Abraham in Genesis 17. God promises Abraham blessings beyond imagination: "And you: You will honor my covenant, you and your descendants, generation after generation'" (Genesis 17:9). For the life lived by Abraham in following God's will, God called Abraham His friend as stated in James 2:21-24, "Wasn't our ancestor Abraham "made right with God by works" when he placed his son Isaac on the sacrificial altar? Isn't it obvious that faith and works are yoked partners, that faith expresses itself in works? That the works are "works of faith"? The full meaning of "believe" in the Scripture sentence, "Abraham believed God and was set right with God," includes his action. It's that mesh of believing and acting that got Abraham named "God's friend." Is it not evident that a person is made right with God not by a barren faith but by faith fruitful in works?"

As others have done, in talking about what their church did to achieve effective results, I want to caution the reader that every church is a fingerprint. The methods and things that will be outlined here are not to be taken as a blueprint for your church. Rather, this story is written to provide inspiration to find your own answers and the motivation to follow through with your own changes.

Retreat

One of the things our church was already doing very well was an annual retreat for our elders and leaders. That retreat was always a few hours away from the church to make sure all distractions were eliminated. During one of those retreats, over five years ago, a lot of attention was given to several popular programs of large ministries like Saddleback and Willow Creek. Nothing really came out of that retreat, however, that resembled a solid move forward. There was a task force appointed to study the situation and make a report back to the session (elected elders of the church). Prior to this event, there were some significant things that had happened in our fellowship.

One of those significant actions included the session commissioning an internally formatted questionnaire to be completed by our membership regarding several church issues being debated by our congregation. One of the main areas addressed was worship. Like any questionnaire, your results will be driven by the way the questions are asked. I don't believe that there was any intention to slant questions; however, the results of the questionnaire caused a serious rift in our congregation. From the results of that questionnaire, the session even voted on a set of rules about what could and could not be done in worship. Not surprisingly, there were no rules about what could and could not be done regarding missions or outreach. The end result was that some left the church, and others who stayed became very complacent about ministry. I would never suggest that a church pass out a questionnaire. Instead, your leadership needs to pray and ask God's direction for your church and then just do it, and be prepared for the feedback, whatever it may be. Again, this effort was a genuine attempt to satisfy everyone by doing what the majority wanted to do.

Several things came out of this, the most important of which was that a lot of prayer was offered up by the congregation, and God heard the cry. My personal prayer was that God would remove anything that stood in the way of ministry in our church—anything. Not long after I said that first prayer, God spoke in a mighty way. He simply said to me, "Bob, get out of the way." I was shocked. I spoke back. "Not me! I can't be the problem! I am one of the ones who recognize that there is a problem! God, you must be mistaken." He wasn't. Not long after that, I resigned as Minister of Music after several years of ministry. I did not leave the church, but just found a seat in the choir for more than five years. During that time, I saw miracle after miracle as God moved people, removed people, and remolded people, including me. It actually became fun to watch.

During that time of reflection and prayer, our session was reformulated, and many very positive actions were taken, most without objection. The first was that those worship rules were thrown out in one single motion. Our leadership meetings became focused on ministry and not money. The meetings actually became shorter, and each meeting started by elders taking turns presenting a devotional. Each meeting was closed with testimonials, prayer requests and a session of prayer. A Session that used to meet every month to micromanage their appointed boards now meets only six times a year and gets more accomplished!

Many other significant events occurred, but one of the most dramatic was the elders' decision to appoint a group to develop a tailored system for providing our congregation with spiritual growth. The end result of that effort yielded *Our Journey*. After just five months in operation, the ministries and studies offered by *Our Journey* involved over forty-five different individuals in a church of about one hundred fifty regular adult attendees. Three years later, over a hundred different members had participated, logging hundreds of hours of study, discussion, and ministry!

The Journey of *Our Journey*

Although the system had immediate effectiveness, *Our Journey* took over two years to develop and implement. A group of motivated individuals agreed to meet for however long it took to find a solution. That group started with a previous effort called *Tusculum U*, whose purpose was to offer specific courses to our church family. It was an academic approach prior to *Our Journey* that never gained any appreciable ground during the first year of its existence.

This new group discussed the needs of ministry within our church and different ways to address those needs. Eventually it was decided that the group should have a mission statement. The system also needed a name, for continuity, that adequately stated our vision and ministry. Sounds easy enough, right? Remember, it took two years! The mission statement alone took three meetings.

Here is the result of many hours of discussions and prayer.

MISSION STATEMENT

To *develop* an atmosphere where dynamic opportunities for Spiritual growth are expected and realized. To *provide* a template of service for all who come to know Christ through direction, study, and encouragement, ultimately allowing for greater spiritual maturity. To *strengthen* leadership through mentoring, knowledge, wisdom, and an understanding of their accountability to God and those whom they serve.

Without a mission statement, you have no way to measure your progress. It is critical that everything you do be measured against your original design. If that does not occur, your church will soon become unfocused, and your efforts will be diluted. This mission statement is critical, and it must be your own. It is one of the very best ways to grow together. While you are welcome to use our statement as a model, you should by no means copy it. It will only work for Tusculum! Besides, if you are not willing to do this first step and lay a basic foundation, you should question your sincerity in addressing the situation.

Curriculum

The next step was to decide what areas to address and how they would be determined. We reviewed everything we were doing at Tusculum. We were amazed by two things: first, the number of things we were doing and second, that the majority of what we were doing was centered on us. Very little could be considered real outreach. Another revealing fact came to our attention. Our foundation was indeed the two morning worship services. Everything centered on those. We had a lot of work to do.

After considerable review, it was determined that our mission statement suggested five areas of ministry. We eventually defined them as the following:

Discovery
Ministry
Mentoring—Two by Two
Understanding
Servant Leadership

Although this list suggests that someone would follow the system in a certain order, we understood that we had a variety of people in our fellowship, all at different places in their Christian growth. For that reason, we made it clear that everyone should evaluate were they were in their Christian life and enter the system at that place. As an object lesson, we used a marquee at a mall. On that marquee, there is a diagram of all of the businesses and an "X" that says, "You are here." Once you determine were you want to go, you can use that map to guide yourself from where you are to where you need to go. We asked our membership to do the same thing. We wanted God to direct them, not a system that was predetermined and set in stone We wanted to meet people where they were, not where we thought they were.

Nine

Our Journey: Relating to the Body

After developing *Our Journey*, we invited every leader in the church to attend our next retreat. Our goal was to offer a description of our current model, explain why it was not working, and present our new approach to ministry with suggestions on how to create a solution. The following is a brief description of our presentation.

Friday Evening:
The following statements were made by the Our Journey team about our agenda and what we hoped to accomplish.

We would cover each of the five sections in summary, not in detail.

> We made it clear that asking questions and making comments was required, however, we asked that everyone be allowed to speak and that no one dominate the discussion.

> We told the group that we would be asking for a commitment at the end of the conference and asked that they begin praying about it immediately.

We hoped to get a consensus that what we, as a church, had been doing was not as effective as it could be.

We would touch lightly on the past, but focus mainly on the future.

We hoped to get acceptance that the model had merit and that they and our church would support it.

We asked for feedback that would allow us to make this everyone's program.

We announced a schedule for launching the program immediately after the retreat.

We hoped to get agreement that the church wanted to grow.

We would be defining the word *intentional* as it applied to ministry.

We wanted everyone to understand that this was a living, changing program.

We would demonstrate that while some may think the use of numbers was inappropriate to measure our success, they would surely be used to measure our failure.

We asked the following questions and asked for feedback:

What have we done in the past that would demonstrate our effectiveness in growing His kingdom that would demand that we continue using those methods?

Why are we now the same size as we were in 1988? (Fourteen years later.)

Does our method—not message need to change?

Do we need to redirect our resources?

Following this introduction, we showed a chart outlining our statistics for attendance, conversions, new members, departing members, and tithes over the past fifteen years. The chart needed no commentary. It spoke volumes.

We made clear that it is normal to get checkups on our bodies, our animals and our cars; so why not our church? We pointed out that this had never been done at a comprehensive level at the Tusculum Church. Instead, review was always reactionary to a negative situation.

We defined our need to look at another approach by comparing changes within the Sears' catalogue over the decades from their first entry into the retail market to the advent of eBay and OverStock.Com to those in the church, noting that everything around us has changed while still producing the same message. We asked why the church was immune.

The following scripture was sited: "They followed a daily discipline of worship in the Temple followed by meals at home, every meal a celebration, exuberant and joyful, as they praised God. People in general liked what they saw. Every day their number grew as God added those who were saved." (Acts 2:46-47). We made sure that folks understood that it is not our job to add to the church. That is His job. Our job is to tend to the flock, both members and non-members, inside the building and outside in the community, especially those who may never darken the door of the church facility.

The first believers experienced a church that was effective in bringing the Gospel to the world. The following scripture was used to reinforce our belief: "The Message is as true among you today as when you first heard it. It doesn't diminish or weaken over time. It's the same all over the world. The Message bears fruit and gets larger and stronger, just as it has in you. From the very first day you heard and recognized the truth of what God is doing, you've been hungry for more." (Colossians 1:5—6).

We defined the early church's four basic functions from Acts 2:41-42: "That day about three thousand took him at his word, were baptized and were signed up. They committed themselves to the **teaching** of the apostles, the life **together**, the common **meal**, and the **prayers** (emphasis added)."

We used the following verse on servant hood, Mark 10:41— 45, "When the other ten heard of this conversation, they lost their tempers with James and John. Jesus got them together to settle things down. 'You've observed how godless rulers throw their weight around,' he said, 'and when people get a little power how quickly it goes to their heads. It's not going to be that way with you. Whoever wants to be great must become a servant. Whoever wants to be first among you must be your slave. That is what the Son of Man has done: He came to serve, not to be served—and then to give away his life in exchange for many who are held hostage'." It is important that we develop a ministry that is not a way of being served, but a place of serving. That service must come from a sense of a calling. If it is determined that a calling has been felt, there should be an obvious feeling of commitment to that calling.

We outlined the church model found throughout Acts:

- It is a church that is led by the Holy Spirit.
- It is a church that's teaching the Word.
- It is a Church that is developing *oneness*, that is fellowship.

We asked the following question, "When you tell someone about our church, what do you say?" We listed phrases such as:

Bible-based preaching
A friendly church
A top-rated daycare
One of the best small church music programs in the city
Celebrating 150 years of ministry to the community

In celebrating baptism, we will sprinkle, immerse, or pour

After listing these items, the group found it interesting what we did *not* tell people about our church; our ministry.

This point, related to familiarity of the congregation with our ministry and our failure to effectively relate that to visitors, was discussed further. An example was given about driving through a large city on a very busy interstate highway. The statement was made that everyone but you seems to know where they are going. The analogy was that most visitors probably feel the same way when visiting our church. Everyone seems to know where they are going except the new folks. If no one stops to give directions to these new folks, they may feel that they are in the way or are not welcome. They don't need someone to tell them where to go, but to take them there. It was agreed that we not only need to provide an effective way for folks to determine where they are physically, but also spiritually. Additionally, they need a road map to get there, but more important, they need a tour guide. Both the method of determining where someone is in their walk and the guide to get them there must be intentional.

We started a discussion on priorities, determining what the group felt was most important and asking if we should be working on our weaknesses or our strengths. Most folks agreed that the need to improve our weaknesses seemed obvious. We suggested that perhaps we should first capitalize on our strengths. It just may be that a weakness in a certain area may indicate that there are too many areas or programs to manage. On the other hand, if you do not correct your weaknesses, you may remain in a rut and not be able to address the void in the lives of those who come to your church in search of answers. They are searching for answers to their needs, not what the church has predetermined it will offer them. This is a discussion that every church should explore in depth. Do not rush this exercise. It will pay deep dividends and take your church places you may not have expected. Remember, it has to do with direction, focus, and expectations.

For the purpose of the following discussion, leadership will be defined as anyone who holds a position in the church for whom a substitute would have to be found should that person not be present. Also included as leaders, for the following discussion, would be anyone who is elected to a position in the church that requires making decisions or accepting responsibility for programs.

The last thing we did in this session was to do some math related to leadership positions in the church. Most have heard of the 80/20 rule, meaning that 20 percent of the people do 80 percent of the work. We wanted to see how that actually played out in our congregation. We listed every leadership position we could think of in our church and were shocked with the number, 103. Next we took our average Sunday morning attendance, 231, and subtracted the elderly, youth, and children. That left 146 adults to fill the 103 positions; however, remember the 80/20 rule. 20 percent of 146 is 29, ironically, the number of people participating in the retreat that year. That got some attention and explained why we had some very worn out leaders!

The real brutality of the above equation is that a smaller church, say, a hundred attendees, would have a need for a similar number of leadership positions. When you do the math, it is no wonder that this size church has so many problems. The main problem is that when people join the church, they are considered fresh meat for the many vacant leadership positions in the church. There is no time to offer them an opportunity to discover what their needs might be, much less time to develop a program that would make such an approach possible. Additionally, there is also no opportunity for them to discover and develop their unique gifts and ultimately use them in ministry to the community. Our research indicated that churches between one hundred and two hundred fifty were the worst possible size. However, on the positive side, a church in this size group could grow to four hundred or six hundred respectively without a great deal of additional physical space. Our church just needed to grow.

Let's triple the regular attendance and do the math to see what happens to the leadership pool.

Regular attendees: 231 × 3 = 693
Minus seniors, youth and children: 693 – 85 × 3 = 438
20 percent rule: 438 × 20% = 87.6 leaders

    Getting back to the church with 231 in attendance, let's do something radical. Let's assume you took a real good look at what you are doing and decided that you really needed to do less and allow for an increase in quality and effectiveness. Let's say you eliminated 25 leadership positions along with the programs or classes they were trying to lead, leaving a need for only 78. Let's do something else rather radical. Let's say you have actually trained each of these folks for ministry and have very specific, written expectations for their service. Let's take a look:

Current situation—103 leadership positions and 29 leaders with little training and no expectations.
Reconfigured—78 leadership positions and 87 leaders with specialized training and high expectations.

    Ask yourself which of these churches is less likely to fail. What changes would have to be made to accommodate tripling the above membership?

Space—multiple services—no building program
Pastor—no change
Staff—one additional young adult pastor (This will take sacrifice and is a great opportunity for stewardship education!)
Utilities—slight increase
Materials—slight increase
Personal commitment or spending time reading God's word, putting together your own system for the spiritual growth of your church body, and inviting people to participate—enormous additional commitment

Nursery—huge increase, but you can draw from new families who have children in this age band.
Sunday School—huge increase, but you can draw from new families who have children in this age band.
(A new young adult pastor can be vital in establishing and managing the last two points above.)

Ask yourself one other question. Which of the two church examples above teaches better stewardship? Now it gets personal when we start talking about *your* money, *your* time and *your* gifts. Remember, this is about individual ministries that collectively grow the church. It is personal.

The Tusculum Church also did a study of staffing needs. We determined that we were properly staffed for our current attendance; however, we also discovered that we were inadequately staffed for growth! In contrast to the unwise use of the concept, "If you build it, they will come," in determining if a church should build on, if you want to have any chance of growing, your church will have to find a way to hire additional staff. This staff is not there to do the work, but to train others to do ministry. This position will likely not work on a volunteer basis. It is far too important a task to expect someone who works forty hours a week and has a family and other obligations to tackle.

This new staff member also goes straight to the heart of *legacy*. Earlier I brought this subject up. The most common problem in small church growth by far is the tradition of waiting until the current pastor dies, retires, or just simply gets worn out and leaves before the church attempts to find another pastor. There is a natural decline in the churches using this traditional process. How much more efficient would it be to have someone already in place to step in when the senior pastor leaves?

This staffing study was accomplished by a different group from the *Our Journey* group. The one common conclusion reached by everyone in this group was that the new position should NOT be called *associate pastor*. Why not? The new position should not be an assistant to the senior pastor. The senior pastor has his own responsibilities. This new position should not be encumbered with anything that distracts from expanding the church to fulfill the new mission statement with special attention to ministry opportunities.. More often than not, those opportunities are going to center around building up your young adult congregation. If the new staff person accomplishes that task, you are going to need several more groups to discuss new needs such as more nursery space, more nursery workers, more Sunday school space, and more Sunday school teachers. But Bob, I thought you said that our church could grow with very little increase in space? I did. You will have to make do, like many of the growing, vibrant churches in your community. Just because you have a new class doesn't mean you need another room complete with new furniture and all the trappings. It demands that you be creative until your growth demands expansion.

Regarding Sunday school growth, your church will likely have the space. There will be additional students added to each class. With that growth in class size, there will be an additional need for more teachers within the same class. When there is no other choice but to build, you will likely also have the funds without borrowing, if the church has planned for the growth from the beginning rather then just reacting when it happens. I am assuming that stewardship education is also a part of your curriculum. Remember the original problem; a small church simply does not have enough bodies. That is what the new staff person is for, training new leaders. Don't worry, it will be fun!

Ten

Our Journey: The Body of Christ in Action

The first step in sharing a vision is to get the listener to recognize a need. If someone cannot envision a void, it will be terribly difficult to get them to see what should replace that void. That was the purpose of the first session of our retreat. It was to create in the fellowship's mind an understanding of the need to do something different and a realization that what was being done, for the most part, was not working. You may have heard that the definition of insanity is doing the same thing over and over and expecting a different result. If that statement is true, it would be safe to say that many churches across this country are on the brink of religious insanity.

In the following two sessions of the retreat, it was vital that we present a practical solution to the problems we presented the evening before. To do that, we took each of the five sections we had determined were needed to fulfill our goal and set out to present them in a concise, understandable manner. This would be terribly difficult for the visionaries in the group who see the vision clearly. Many visionaries get very frustrated at this point because not everyone else can see what they see because they are usually way ahead of the group in developing the concept. The visionary stands on top of the mountain waving to the crowd below to come on up, never understanding why the crowd remains in the valley shaking their heads and staring in disbelief at the crazy person standing on the mountain waving at them.

That is why you need some grounded individuals involved in your task force or study team. It gives the crazy people waving their arms a little credibility. Grounded individuals give balance to the equation. One word of caution: folks who are grounded are like anchors; properly placed in the process, they perform a very useful function. If you never bring up the anchor though, you are not likely to make much progress. At this point in our journey, it was time to raise the anchors and sail full steam ahead.

It was important in the following two presentations that we distinguish very clearly between a vision and a goal. Ken Blanchard and Phil Hodges have a great definition of these two terms in their book, *Lead Like Jesus (8)*. I strongly recommend that you read this book. The authors define a vision as having no beginning or end. It is something that is bigger than those who are experiencing the vision. A vision, by definition, has no limits. It just is. A goal, however, has a definite beginning and end. A goal can be seen, felt, heard, and experienced. Goals have to be changed because we reach them. A vision may never be fully realized in the visionary's lifetime.

Following are definitions of the five areas we emphasized and how we presented them on the second day of the retreat.

Discovery

We determined that there is a time in the life of every Christian when the believer needs to search their mind, soul, and heart. The contemporary term for this is *seeker*. Modern Christianity has seeker services, seeker literature, seeker praise songs, seeker small groups, seeker jewelry, seeker coffee shops, seeker, seeker, seeker. It is apparent that most small churches do not adopt this concept because they see it as a "big" church phenomenon. Nothing could be further from the truth. Being a seeker simply means you are on a search for God, and once you find Him, will seek His purpose and direction for your life ministry. We chose to call this *discovery*.

We compiled a list of prompts and study topics to be explored while in the discovery stage. Those included:

What have I done by accepting Jesus as my personal savior?

What does it mean to be a Christian?

What does it mean to be Cumberland Presbyterian?

Basic history of the Christian faith

Basic history and current information on the Cumberland Presbyterian denomination

Exploring spiritual gifts: what they are and why we have them

Identifying one's spiritual gifts and ways to use them in the Body of Christ

The other thing that we came to understand was that there are people in our church who have been believers for many years that never took this journey. Perhaps it was not available (most likely), or there was never an expectation that they participate, or they chose not to participate. Whatever the reason may have been, we wanted to make sure that this group felt welcome and knew that it would be in the Body of Christ's best interest for them to make that journey. This was an opportunity to lovingly express expectations that members continually seek spiritual growth.

One of our mottos for this section was a result of our teams research and application of what we discovered, "God doesn't *call* the qualified; He qualifies the *called*." Moses was not qualified when God appeared to him in the burning bush. God spent the next forty years certifying him. It was our team's hope that people would understand that the call on their lives came first. God doesn't use resumes.

Whoever is in charge of this Discovery module needs to be committed to the task. This will require a great deal of research, patience, and a grounded, living faith. It should *not* be the pastor, although the pastor's input and support is critical. The pastor is in a unique position to stress expectations regarding participation in this program from the pulpit. Without that support your program will not be successful.

Again, although this seems to be an obvious starting place for everyone, it may not be for some who initially feel that they are beyond this point. If the rest of the program goes as planned, many will eventually feel a need to back up and attend these classes.

Ministry

Ministry is a very general term. It is so general that we did a quick survey of what we called ministry at Tusculum. We listed over twenty-five items. Some of these where ministry, as we now define it, but most were just things we did. Practically everything was pointed inward; we did it for those who were already in the church. I doubt Jesus would consider much of what we call ministry to be faithfully fulfilling His great commandment. Our objective in this session was to get the listener to see the direction of ministry as it was and then how it should be. To illustrate this, we put a GPS satellite image of our property on the screen. Over that, we placed the titles of all of the things we were doing. The illustration was obvious; we were pointed inward.

In an effort to illustrate the problem, we used a diagram from www.venus.walagata.com that shows the priorities of failing churches. This is illustrated by a tiered pyramid. At the base of this pyramid, forming the foundation of the church is the weekend worship service. Everything else sits on top of that supporting foundation. At the top of this pyramid are the missions, existing almost as an afterthought. True missions look outward and are a ministry that is done outside the walls of the church. Worship looks inward and is molded to fit the needs of those who are already attending. Worship doesn't have to be that way, but if it is the foundation of your ministry, it is unlikely that worship will change. It also accounts for all the friction encountered in most churches when someone "messes" with tradition. If a church will reverse the pyramid and make missions their foundation, changes in worship will be a natural transition, not a wedge. I define the problem this way: In the first century, God's people became known as "people of the way." Today, we are known as people of the schedule.

I mentioned earlier Jesus' personal touch as explained by Jim Henderson. This is where we used that reference in the retreat. Consider the following research. The gospels record one hundred thirty-two interactions Jesus had with people. Six were in the temple, four in the synagogue, and one hundred twenty-two were out with the people in the mainstream of life. It raises the question, What did Jesus think about worship inside the walls and ministry outside the walls? If we are to take the name *Christian*, meaning to be like Christ, maybe we need to reexamine our attitude towards and definitions of worship and ministry (missions).

We did not want to create a problem without solutions, so we also outlined seventeen possible ministries both in and out of town. We also praised the group for those few ministries that were already being accomplished outside the church. We left the group with a final thought. The *ministry first* approach creates a common goal, reaching out to the world. It changes the mind-set to, "We are the church during the week" from, "We are the church on Sunday morning in worship." Further, this *ministry first* approach suggests that the church then gets together for worship on the weekends to celebrate their ministry during the past week, not to perform a ritual."

Mentoring—Two by Two

Our task team came to an awesome conclusion: spiritual mentoring was vital to the growth of the Christian faith. If that were true, why did it have a backseat in modern Christianity? It was time to move to the front of the bus. Consider the following verse from Ecclesiastes 4:9-12:

"It's better to have a partner than go it alone. Share the work, share the wealth. And if one falls down, the other helps, But if there's no one to help, tough! Two in a bed warm each other. Alone, you shiver all night. By yourself you're unprotected. With a friend you can face the worst. Can you round up a third? A three-stranded rope isn't easily snapped."

It is a fact that two people together can do more work than three working individually.

So, what is mentoring? From birth to death, our lives are connected. The mentoring process begins the day you are born. We are all mentored by someone or something, a parent, grandparent, teacher, friend, or the television. There is a natural process in life that we, as humans, often disrupt, trying to substitute something better. In the spring, you will often see a bird flying rather oddly through the air. If you look closely, you will see a small spec beside it. It is the baby, learning by example from the parent. To our knowledge, there is no bird language, so all learning is by visual example. Unfortunately, in our age, that visual example is often broken because parents, for many reasons, decide that everyone will be better off if divorce is the ultimate outcome. Regardless of how much justification the parents dream up, their children are in for an uncertain future with a distorted, unnatural visual example. The church has developed much the same attitude. When new people come into the church, either as new believers or by transferring from some other fellowship, they are often left without any guidance or source of knowledge about the faith, the church, and most important, the ministry. That is why the New Testament Church grew so strong so quickly. The element of one-on-one ministry was part of the norm for the church in Acts.

There are very few things that we are able to do on an individual basis that would not improve when shared with someone else. Mentoring, however, does not mean the same thing to everyone. Let's look at a few words that are considered synonyms.

Coach may come to mind. Many people, especially children and teenagers, are molded by a sports coach. That is where many learn discipline for the first time. What does a coach do? They explain how the game is played, determine who plays when, and comes up with a strategy for winning. If we take this as our definition, it probably does not cover *mentor*.

A *discipler* may be considered one who makes disciples. Christ's command to us was to go out and make disciples, a worthy charge for all of us. In one sense, *discipling* is simply introducing others to Christ. In another sense it could mean what you do for them after they have met the Savior. This may be a little closer to the definition of a mentor. However, it is still pretty much a one-way relationship.

The term *spiritual guide* could mean several things, some not as appealing as we would like, for instance, a New Age guru leading you on a journey through the wonders of the universe to get in touch with the one true god—you. The other problem with this term is that it sets up the *spiritual guide* for failure. It suggests that the guide is someone who has arrived and has all of the answers. Again, this is a unidirectional journey, usually in the wrong direction.

If we look at the pure definition of the terms *spiritual* and *mentor* we find that the definition of spiritual, as defined in *The Free Dictionary by Farlex on-line*, is, "concerned with or affecting the soul, pertaining to God, belonging to a church or religious organization." On the other hand, a mentor is, "a wise and trusted teacher." Proverbs 13:14 tells us that, "The teaching of the wise is a fountain of life, so, no more drinking from death-tainted wells!"

Perhaps we need to combine these two terms into spiritual

mentoring which would give us the following picture of a lifelong relationship, in which a mentor helps a apprentice reach his or her God-given potential. It is more a, "how can I help you?" relationship rather than a "what can I teach you?" relationship. It becomes a two-way dialogue.

Mentors should expect the ones they are mentoring to come back from ministry beat-up emotionally, confused, frustrated, and disappointed. The first task of a mentor is to lead people into ministry. The second job is to listen, not act. Should the person be totally prepared before they are lead into a particular ministry opportunity? No. There are some things that you cannot teach. They have to be experienced and then explained. If everyone were totally prepared for ministry and perfect in their follow-through, there wouldn't be much need for mentors. However, there is not much danger in mentors becoming extinct. They are, however, often overlooked.

Ecclesiastes chapter four offers four principles for building a strong mentoring program. Please get your Bible and follow along.

Efficiency—They have a good return for their work. As we mentioned, two working together can accomplish more than a greater number of individuals working apart.

Encouragement—They pick each other up. Many generals have used as their motto, "Leave no soldier behind." That should certainly be true of Christian warfare. Unfortunately, it is said that Christians are the only ones who kick their wounded. There are several reasons for that reaction. Some are so Heavenly-minded that they fail to see a hurting friend at their feet and trip over them. They have their heads in the clouds looking for that perfect place they have been promised. Christ told us to look up, for our redemption was drawing near. He did not say to continue to look up and ignore the world around you. Remember, there will be a very loud trumpet (not piano and organ) that will blast when he arrives. He will get your attention, so be alert to those around you. You will not be left behind.

Exhortation—They keep one another warm. I am a product of the sixties and seventies music scene. One of the popular groups of that era was called, "Three Dog Night." Growing up, I never bothered to ask where the name came from. After all, "it was about the music man." Years later I heard the following story (I cannot confirm the story, but it sounds good.) One of the band members was in Alaska on a cold night prior to the group becoming popular. He asked how cold it was and was told by one of the locals that it was a *three dog night*. Curious, he asked what that meant. He was told that it was a common practice for dogsled drivers to use their animals' body heat to stay warm at night as they slept. The driver would determine how cold it was and would use a certain number of dogs for that temperature. That evening, it was a three dog night. The name obviously stuck.

Warmth comes in many different forms. The warmth of a smile, a mentor saying "job well done," a hug when nothing seems to be working, a hand reaching down to pick us up when we have fallen. Maybe even a kick in the rear when we are slothful if nothing else seems to work. A mentor has the ability to measure the temperature and determine how many dogs need to be brought into the tent. A good one can do it without a thermometer.

Energy or Strength—They defend one another against the enemy. A good question would be who is the enemy? The scripture is clear that Satan is sneaking around trying to find those who he can devour. That sounds like an enemy to me. However, as usual our worst enemies are not the obvious ones. Your enemy might be procrastination, substance abuse, gambling, laziness, pornography, pride, lust, selfishness, or any of the seven deadly sins. A mentor will make you accountable. That is one of the main parts of the twelve-step system in AA. Recovering alcoholics must realize that they cannot do it alone. They need someone to call who has been through it and understands; someone who will sympathize, but still hold them to their promise. They realize the importance of truth and accountability. Truth creates energy, and accountability produces strength.

Ecclesiastes four goes even further. A "cord of three strands" is even stronger. If two together can do more than two individuals, what could three together accomplish? Jesus followed this model in ministry. He first started with the crowd, ministering to groups through the spoken word. Later, he would choose from that large group the twelve disciples who would become His top class. From that group, He would rely on three to be His special students, Peter, James, and John. He would be a mentor to them, and later, they would be support for each other.

Our church ministry is similarly constructed. The crowd—those who attend our weekend services—represent the group at large, the masses that Jesus preached to on the roads and the hillsides. From that group you will attain various levels of commitment. Some will be seeking spiritual nourishment, others will just be curious, and others will be there out of some sense of legal fulfillment.

From that group will emerge a smaller group, either elected or appointed, that will attempt to lead the larger group. This represents the disciples chosen by Jesus. Again, there will be varying degrees of understanding and commitment within this group. This is where most religious organizations falter and begin to break down. The reason they break down is that the pastor fails to complete the example of Christ in becoming a mentor to those who exemplify the touch of God in their lives. This small group never develops past the level of commitment of the larger group. There is never an opportunity for these individuals to gain a deeper understanding of God's call in their life, so they have no chance to progress.

If the pastor does not step up to the plate, the local church is doomed. On occasion, those special folks are so hungry for more that they actively seek fellowship from each other and ultimately demand it from their pastor. More likely, if guidance is not offered by their pastor, they find it somewhere else rather than asking him for help. In the latter case, those individuals may leave the church and take with them the seeds of growth that could have been used for a dying congregation. This often happens quietly, and it is years later that the church looks around and discovers that somewhere along the journey, all of their assets disappeared. At that point it is tragically too late. Only a miracle could save a church at this point in their journey.

This third strand, the core of the church—made up of its current and future leaders, the ones who want to go deeper, the ones with a passion to grow spiritually, but most importantly the ones who have a desire to help others grow in Christ and to reach out to the lost—must be mentored. This group needs someone to be honest with them, to be the voice of reason and a spiritual mentor.

Again, the role of a mentor is to hold your feet to the fire, make you accountable. It takes someone who can see your potential, someone who can discern your strengths, someone who can help you overcome your weaknesses. This is a partnership of trust.

We identified the following as possible ways to begin mentoring: small groups, elder assistant programs (matching young and old, harnessing the wisdom of the retired), two by two visits, and placing those who recently lost loved ones or who had gone through a debilitating disease with someone who has walked that path.

We ended this section with the following verse, Galatians 6:1-3, "Live creatively, friends. If someone falls into sin, forgivingly restore him, saving your critical comments for yourself. You might be needing forgiveness before the day's out. Stoop down and reach out to those who are oppressed. Share their burdens, and so complete Christ's law. If you think you are too good for that, you are badly deceived." Based on this verse we expressed to the group that Christ desires for us to have a bonding of the heart, moving forward eye to eye, back to back, and shoulder to shoulder.

If this is properly done, maybe you can avoid the following phrase, "I don't have time to serve anyone. I'm a leader."

Understanding

Up to this point we have identified three areas of concentration for this ministry approach, Discovery, Ministry and Mentoring Two-by-Two. The fourth area we identified emphasizes a Christian's need to develop a deeper understanding of God's word and apply the principles found there to spiritual growth.

Colossians 1:3-5 says, "Our prayers for you are always spilling over into thanksgivings. We can't quit thanking God our Father and Jesus our Messiah for you! We keep getting reports on your steady faith in Christ, our Jesus, and the love you continuously extend to all Christians. The lines of purpose in your lives never grow slack, tightly tied as they are to your future in heaven, kept taut by hope."

Paul, more than all the other writers of the New Testament, realized the importance of developing a deeper understanding of God's message. As with Paul's personal journey, this deeper relationship does not happen by accident. It must be intentional, and a follower of Christ must make that journey a passion.

Perhaps the best place to begin is by defining the word *understanding*. The Greek Word used in Colossians 1:9, is *sunesis*. This is translated in Thayer's Greek-English Lexicon of the New Testament as "a running together, a flowing together with two things, knowledge and understanding." In much of the New Testament, the verb, *understand,* is considered a moral and spiritual issue, not an intellectual issue. The question then is how are we to have a spiritual openness to the responses of God to us? The answer is through fellowship with God the Father, God the Son, and God the Holy Spirit. God is difficult to understand even while in a personal relationship. How can someone begin to understand with no relationship at all?

The first way to obtain this understanding and fellowship with God the Father begins with the idea of *agape* love. 1 John 4:7—10 says, "My beloved friends, let us continue to love each other since love comes from God. Everyone who loves is born of God and experiences a relationship with God. The person who refuses to love doesn't know the first thing about God, because God is love—so you can't know him if you don't love. This is how God showed his love for us: God sent his only Son into the world so we might live through him. This is the kind of love we are talking about—not that we once upon a time loved God, but that he loved us and sent his Son as a sacrifice to clear away our sins and the damage they've done to our relationship with God." Therefore, God is love, and love can rest or lay dormant until it is returned. In order for us to understand God's will for our lives, we must return His love for us. We all deserve His wrath because of our sin and disobedience, but He has showered upon us His grace, and he has covered and purified us by the blood of His only son. Further, we find in 1 John 1:6-7, "If we claim that we experience a shared life with him and continue to stumble around in the dark, we're obviously lying through our teeth—we're not living what we claim. But if we walk in the light, God himself being the light, we also experience a shared life with one another, as the sacrificed blood of Jesus, God's Son, purges all our sin."

Secondly, we must establish fellowship with God the Son, Jesus Christ. In order to do this, we must always acknowledge that He came in the flesh. He was and is fully human and fully divine.

In this session, we sited the Nicene Creed, written in 325 A.D. which begins by saying this about Jesus Christ: "We believe in one Lord, Jesus Christ, the only Son of God, eternally begotten of the Father, God from God, Light from Light, true God from true God, begotten, not made, one in Being with the Father."

Thirdly, we must be in fellowship with the third person of the Godhead, the Holy Spirit. Sometimes we all feel like we are one of the Ephesians in Acts 19:1—2: "Now, it happened that while Apollos was away in Corinth, Paul made his way down through the mountains, came to Ephesus, and happened on some disciples there. The first thing he said was, "Did you receive the Holy Spirit when you believed? Did you take God into your mind only, or did you also embrace him with your heart? Did he get inside you?"

We felt that our ability to understand what God has given us through His Holy Spirit was outlined by Paul as he said to the church at Corinth in 1 Corinthians 2:10—16: "The Spirit, not content to flit around on the surface, dives into the depths of God, and brings out what God planned all along. Who ever knows what you're thinking and planning except you yourself? The same with God—except that he not only knows what he's thinking, but he lets us in on it. God offers a full report on the gifts of life and salvation that he is giving us. We don't have to rely on the world's guesses and opinions. We didn't learn this by reading books or going to school; we learned it from God, who taught us person-to-person through Jesus, and we're passing it on to you in the same firsthand, personal way."

The unspiritual self, just as it is by nature, can't receive the gifts of God's Spirit. There's no capacity for them. They seem like so much silliness. Spirit can be known only by spirit—God's Spirit and our spirits in open communion. Spiritually alive, we have access to everything God's Spirit is doing, and can't be judged by unspiritual critics. Isaiah's question, "Is there anyone around who knows God's Spirit, anyone who knows what he is doing?" has been answered: Christ knows, and we have Christ's Spirit."

Paul had continued in 1 Corinthians 2:14-16, "The unspiritual self, just as it is by nature, can't receive the gifts of God's Spirit. There's no capacity for them. They seem like so much silliness. Spirit can be known only by spirit—God's Spirit and our spirits in open communion. Spiritually alive, we have access to everything God's Spirit is doing, and can't be judged by unspiritual critics. Isaiah's question, "Is there anyone around who knows God's Spirit, anyone who knows what he is doing?" has been answered: Christ knows, and we have Christ's Spirit." So by growing and establishing fellowship with God the Father, the Son, and the Holy Spirit, we can take preliminary steps in *Our Journey*. This became the basis of our section on understanding.

Out of this came seven expectations for ourselves and our members as we began *Our Journey* in understanding and developing a deeper relationship with Him.

The First Expectation—Our Journey's first expectation is simply a deep spiritual relationship with Jesus Christ as Lord and Savior. It is a question that should be asked of all within the Body of Christ, His church: "Are you where you want to be in your relationship with God?" We ended each of these seven expectations with a statement: "As we begin our journey together, we have help and encouragement for you."

The Second Expectation—Every member of the Tusculum church will be accountable, first to the Lord and second to a specific chosen group. We asked if the participants were accountable in their spiritual lives.

The Third Expectation—To learn what your natural and spiritual gifts and talents are and how to use them to the honor and the glory of God. We asked if the participants knew what their gifts and talents were.

The Fourth Expectation—After learning and understanding what different gifts and talents you have been given for God's glory and honor, we expect you to give of these natural talents and spiritual gifts as members of the body of Christ.

A few years ago at Tusculum, we undertook a study of *How Much Is Enough* by Larry Burkett. During this study, we learned to tithe our time and our other natural gifts and talents. That expectation continues to be a part of our Christian walk and our spiritual maturity and growth. After this study, there was an acceptance by most of our members regarding this vital part of our spiritual growth.

Our God, who is the Creator of heaven and earth, always deserves the best of what we have. As Paul says to us and to the Romans in the chapter 12, verses 1 and 2,

"So here's what I want you to do, God helping you: Take your everyday, ordinary life—your sleeping, eating, going-to-work, and walking-around life—and place it before God as an offering. Embracing what God does for you is the best thing you can do for him. Don't become so well-adjusted to your culture that you fit into it without even thinking. Instead, fix your attention on God. You'll be changed from the inside out. Readily recognize what he wants from you, and quickly respond to it. Unlike the culture around you, always dragging you down to its level of immaturity, God brings the best out of you, develops well-formed maturity in you."

We asked all participants if they were ready to sacrifice.

The Fifth Expectation—Each member of our family should develop a consistent daily Bible study and prayer life. It is amazing how often we overlook this simple, vital part of our daily growth.

The Sixth Expectation—To begin or continue sharing the good news of Jesus Christ with the lost in a world. We stressed that they should not focus on the popular phrase, "What would Jesus do," as important as that might be, but rather, "Do what Jesus did."

The Seventh Expectation—We expect our part of the body of Christ at Tusculum to become "servant leaders." This was a surprising concept that was foreign to most who heard it. It became the motto for our last section of this ministry, Servant Leadership. This will be discussed a little later.

We made it clear that as we continue to develop and grow in these areas of *understanding*, there may be other spiritual expectations, such as working on our spiritual discipline, which eventually could be incorporated into this section of *Our Journey*. We knew that the God of all creation expects us to fulfill our responsibilities as His adopted children.

One of those responsibilities is to become the spiritual person that God wants us to be. In order to do that, we encouraged our congregation to begin thinking with the mind and attitude of Christ as described in Philippians 2:5—8: "Think of yourselves the way Christ Jesus thought of himself. He had equal status with God but didn't think so much of himself that he had to cling to the advantages of that status no matter what. Not at all. When the time came, he set aside the privileges of deity and took on the status of a slave, became human! Having become human, he stayed human. It was an incredibly humbling process. He didn't claim special privileges. Instead, he lived a selfless, obedient life and then died a selfless, obedient death—and the worst kind of death at that—a crucifixion." We stressed that we are not to be enablers, facilitators, or role models, but are to announce how Jesus is still leading God's people out of the slavery of legalism and fear and into His love and grace.

In summary of *understanding*, our lives should show how to learn through the knowledge of who we are in Jesus and how to overcome the "isms" of our lives: fatalism, defeatism, accidentalism, and incidentalism. We ask if the participants were ready to overcome these and other *isms* in their lives.

Understanding is an opportunity to learn how to develop our spiritual life and grow closer to God by continuing biblical study and an active prayer life. *Our Journey* is an opportunity to see that God is continually working on all of us individually so that we collectively can become the "light on the hill" for the lost. This is accomplished not only through reflection, meditation, and study, but by another very important part of *understanding*—doing. All the knowledge and study are not worth the effort if we just sit idle, neglecting to put our beliefs into practice in the world, as Jesus did.

We offered a place to start by providing spiritual tools. Some of those tools included continuing to pray for God's guidance while we developed small group ministries, especially outside of the comfort of our buildings. This would be accomplished by establishing smaller Bible studies in homes and strengthening our Sunday school and Wednesday night Bible studies. We decided to broaden our choice of classes and presentation methods. We did not replace the traditional Bible Study program, but added to it additional opportunities, incorporating elders and other teachers. These classes and study groups included studies such as The Beatitudes and the Book of John. Topical studies were added such as Grace, Faith, Salvation, Sanctification, and Justification.

Servant Leadership

Are leaders born, appointed, elected, or developed? Consider what was suggested by John Maxwell in his book, *The 21 Irrefutable Laws of Leadership*, "He who thinks he leads but has no followers is simply out taking a walk." There are two kinds of leaders, executive and servant. Let's explore the difference. Bill Gates is a perfect example of an executive leader. Mother Teresa is a perfect example of a servant leader. Servant leadership doesn't get much press. Looking at the life of Moses and his taking the life of an Egyptian guard, we find this verse in Exodus 2:14: "The man shot back: "Who do you think you are, telling us what to do? Are you going to kill me the way you killed that Egyptian?" Then Moses panicked: "Word's gotten out—people know about this."

As an executive leader, this action of Moses did get a lot of press. In fact the scripture goes on to say, "and then he ran!" Like most leaders who are in high positions, Moses feared for his reputation and his life. The most desperate, desolate place for any leader is in retreat. Thankfully, God was not through with Moses. He was about to be introduced to a new kind of leadership. Uncharacteristic of corporate leadership, his transition would take decades and would come from some very unlikely sources.

What did Moses do? He became still and listened for direction. He would eventually charge forward, but with a different perspective and purpose. This man who couldn't even do a good job of burying one Egyptian later succeeded in burying an Egyptian army!

So what made the difference? The following was written by George W. Truett in Powhatten James: "The man of God must have *insight* into things Spiritual. He must be able to *see* the mountains filled with the horses and chariots or fire; He must be able to *interpret* that which is written by the finger of God on the walls of conscience; He must be able to *translate* the signs of the times into terms of their Spiritual meaning; He must be able to *draw* aside, now and then, the curtain of things material and let mortals glimpse the Spiritual Glories which crown the Mercy Seat of God."

One last thought about Moses and servant leadership. He led from within the people, not above them; this is the true definition of servant leadership.

You cannot determine the extent of your ability to lead until you take the advice of the Psalmist in Psalm 46:8-10: "Attention, all! See the marvels of God! He plants flowers and trees all over the earth, bans war from pole to pole, breaks all the weapons across his knee. Step out of the traffic! Take a long, loving look at me, your High God, above politics, above everything." Christ taught this by example in John 21:15—17. Jesus tells Peter three times to be a servant. Peter would later understand the significance of that moment on two different occasions. Once, before Jesus appeared to him and others at the Tiberius Sea, Peter would remember the rooster crowing at his denial of Jesus, and later, at Pentecost, Jesus' words would pierce his heart again. Peter began his transformation from executive to servant with these words in John 21:15—17. That transformation sent Peter on a journey that would eventually cost him his life.

This segment of *Our Journey* is an observation post, a learning station. This segment of *Our Journey* is the fruit of spiritual growth. This segment of *Our Journey* should be everyone's goal—to lead wherever God directs—first by example, last by commitment to finish what you start.

Classes for this series on servant leadership initially included: The Life of Peter, Paul…a Man of Grit and Grace, Listening…a Servants Ear, God's Credit Card, and Seven Steps to Spiritual Growth. Later sessions included the *Jesus Style,* and *Do You Have Enough Faith to be an Atheist?*

Earlier we mentioned that Mother Teresa is a perfect example of a servant leader. We also remarked that servant leadership doesn't get much press. Maybe that is because their perspective doesn't always fit the world view. That is clear in one of Mother Teresa's quotes.

People are often unreasonable, illogical, and even self-centered.
Forgive them anyway.
If you are kind, people may accuse you of selfish, ulterior motives.
Be kind anyway.
If you are successful, you will win some false friends and some true enemies.
Succeed anyway.
If you are honest and frank, people may cheat you.
Be honest and frank anyway.
What you spend years building, someone could destroy in one night.
Build anyway.
If you find serenity and happiness, they may be jealous.
Be happy anyway.
The good you do today, people will often forget tomorrow.
Do good anyway.
Give the world the best you have, and it may never be enough.
Give the best you've got anyway.
You see, in the final analysis, it is between you and God.
It was never between you and them anyway.

These five sections have become the backbone of training and growth for our church. It did not replace anything already in existence. However, the structure gave the church enough flexibility to design many new approaches that can be adjusted according to the needs of our community and those who come into our church for the first time. It has taken years for this program to get off the ground, and it will take more time for it to become effective. The blessing is that we can already see positive results from our efforts to listen to God's guidance. Our church knows that God recognizes our effort to make ourselves available to Him for His purpose in our community and the world. God will use us because we are ready.

Eleven

The Pastor

I could get in a lot of trouble in this chapter. To some, this is an untouchable topic by a layman. Regardless of what might be said here, it will be taken by most as criticism. However, nothing could be further from the truth. This book would be meaningless if this subject were left untouched. Let me begin by saying my comments are in no way directed at any particular pastor, in particular my pastor, who has dedicated his life to God and our church over the past three decades and more. God has blessed him and our church because he accepted His call to Tusculum.

In a modern church, a pastor is the central focus of everything that happens. If the pastor is not supportive of a program or ministry, it has very little chance of succeeding. I have stated this to our pastor on numerous occasions, and he disagreed. Recently, however, he has come to believe that it is true. This fact is both the blessing and the curse of church growth and decay. While a church can manage and maintain without a pastor, it cannot grow without one. That places an enormous burden on the pastor and the congregation to seek God's guidance in combining the pastor's vision and the vision of the church.

If the vision and mission of the church and the pastor are to have a vibrant Sunday morning worship service, and everything else is subordinate to that endeavor, both the church and the pastor have already started to decline. Let's take a quick look at Jesus as our pastor.

How many sermons are recorded in scripture that were delivered by Jesus?

On the other hand, how many personal encounters were recorded in scripture related to Jesus ministry?

It would appear that Jesus' main focus was on the twelve. He must have spent hours, even days or months with these chosen leaders, the ones who would carry on His message after He died. In fact, it is believed that one of the main reasons He chose these people was to leave behind a group of authentic followers who could carry on His message. These were people who could continue to walk with and train others, people whom the growing Christian community would respect. With this example firmly in mind, ask yourself how most pastors are forced to do just the opposite, distracted from teaching and ministering to find time to coddle some in the congregation just to keep peace.

What if a pastor's first priority was to spend days, even months, closely working with and training elders and deacons in the church body? What if the pastor didn't have a good delivery on Sunday morning, but was able to train his leadership to do as Christ commanded? Would it make a difference in your church? Yes, it would.

Although I am not a pastor, nor am I ordained, I have spent over forty-years working beside these men and women of God. I have seen the tears of joy flowing freely and I have seen the bomb go off. I have seen people called into ministry who never make it past the first hurdle. God has given me an interesting spot in life from which to observe the pastorate. Here are a few of the stumbling blocks I have recorded in my memory from past experiences.

Legalism

Of all the things that crowd out ministry, legalism wins all awards. Oddly enough, it is the same thing that Jesus fought against His entire time on Earth. From my observations, I can only speculate that pastors fall into this pit for the following reasons:

Power—This is hard to understand since Jesus said all power is mine under heaven and earth. Nevertheless, some pastors seem to want to run everything. They have to be on every committee, be in every discussion, approve every motion, and get feedback on hallway conversations. More than power, I have sensed a control problem. If this is a problem for you or your pastor, fix it. Don't try to soft pedal the approach. This kind of attitude will only postpone any hope you have for growth.

Insecurity—I have witnessed pastors that seem to have a permanent look of fear on their face. They have an unnatural desire to please the congregation. They dread every upcoming Session meeting or congregational meeting for fear that they did or said something wrong, and there will be untold consequences. I encourage you to give this pastor the benefit of the doubt. Meet with them. Give them an opportunity to seek counseling if necessary. Above all, pray for and with them. However, they should know that their insecurity is a stumbling block to the church. It must go away or the pastor should resign. God still performs miracles.

A Deranged Sense of Theology—This problem can be disastrous. Here is the problem. When pastors go through seminary, they are intentionally exposed to some rather weird theology. This is to make them think, not endorse it. Unfortunately, if the pastors are not well-grounded and are prone to questioning certain areas of their faith, the exposure in seminary becomes real. The result is a theology that can rip a church apart, maybe so badly that it will never recover.

Tradition—This could be the ten ton anchor on a rowboat. I have absolutely no problem with a pastor wearing a robe. I have no problem with a pastor wanting to use liturgy in every service. What I have observed, however, is that some pastors wear robes and insist on inflexible worship styles because it is just the way you do things. In his book, *The Jesus Style* by Gayle Erwin, there are two statements that stand out to me. First, Mr. Erwin states that whatever the church or an individual makes more important than everything else becomes the object that is worshiped.

The second statement was that Jesus' coming to earth was the equivalent of wrapping love with flesh.[14]

If wearing a robe is mandatory, does it become the object of worship? If not, ask the pastor to consider not wearing it for a period of time. If liturgy is not being worshiped, ask that it not be incorporated for a period of time. During that period, observe if the pastor is uncomfortable without a robe or using non-liturgical worship presentations. If the pastor cannot get past that, there is a problem. Again, there is absolutely nothing wrong with either of these. Conversely, a pastor can also make wearing an Hawaiian shirt the object of their worship. The question is what is being worshiped? If Jesus is love wrapped in flesh, how can anyone be a traditionalist? How can anyone defend a position of tradition regarding the church? They cannot. Remember what was said earlier. Ask yourself the question, what have we been doing so right that could justify continuing in the same manner? If you always do what you have always done, you will get what you have always gotten. Is your church satisfied with that result? Are you?

Job Security—We have all worked with folks who create situations to secure the need for their services. Unknowingly to the congregation, many pastors may not suggest support staff because the person hired might do a better job than they are doing. They are simply afraid that they may be hiring their replacement. Guess what? That is the idea. Job security is training your replacement. It might take a year or it might take twenty years. Speak with your pastor about their legacy. Help them create a legacy before they leave; for whatever reason.

Personality Defect—Most churches eventually discover this problem. Unfortunately, it is usually too late when it is finally confronted. No one gets along with everyone. If your pastor is combative or defensive, there is probably a reason. It takes an understanding church to work through this, but it is worth the effort. A pastor with that much passion can become a significant force for church growth. Perhaps the following questions will bring to mind things you have observed about your pastor. Perhaps these questions will make you think about things you never thought about and create in your heart a desire to turn the tables and allow you to begin ministering to your pastor.

When was the last time you asked your pastor how he was doing physically? When was the last time you inquired about the health and wellbeing of the pastor's family? When is the last time you walked up to your pastor and asked if you could pray for him, right there, right then? Do you offer an opportunity for your pastor to receive counseling? Who pastors your pastor? Do you provide your pastor time to be away from the pulpit and more importantly the whining of some and the overwhelming needs of others he must listen to in the church office and privately in his office week after week? Chances are, if you had to put up with what the average pastor has to deal with, you would also have a personality defect. This can also occur because, as was earlier outlined, the church expects the pastor to do all of the "spiritual stuff." By simply working through these kinds of issues, your church could be set on fire for growth! Try it.

Pressure from Higher Church Courts—I saved this one for last because that is where it deserves to be. Some pastors, when away from their church environment, forget their calling when given high church duties. These individuals can become enamored with this supposedly "higher" calling. There is a tendency for them to stay in this environment because they get some personal satisfaction out of sending down rulings to lower church courts. You say, "Bob, you have got to be kidding. This doesn't go on in the twenty-first century…does it?" Ah, yes it does. It has gone on for centuries. This is where the problem began for denominations. It is also where it can end. You don't fix this by standing on the sidelines throwing rocks. You fix this by becoming involved in your church and it's affiliated denomination. You get elected or appointed to these higher courts or boards and find out first hand what is going on. Just as Christ did, you fix this from within the walls. A word of caution, make sure your own house is in order before you start cleaning someone else's. Don't become part of the problem.

If your church is to grow and be the mission's headquarters for your community and the world, it must begin and end with the pastor. In the middle are the laymen. Working together in one accord, walking hand in hand, there is nothing that is impossible for a fellowship of believers. If you take on this challenge, you are not creating something new, just reviving what Christ taught over two thousand years ago. Will you, maybe for the very first time, consider your faith to be the most important thing you have? Will you face the eastern sky and without a doubt in your mind know that Christ could break through the clouds at any moment and call you to His kingdom? Come on. Get together with your pastor and a few folks in your fellowship and begin praying about your church.

Twelve

In Conclusion of Things

Over the last two years, while composing this book, I have often wondered at what point this subject became so important to me that I would give it such a prominent place on my priority list. It wasn't when I was in high school. At that time, I was consumed with sports, music, girls, cars, and just going about the business of being a teenager. I was, however, deeply committed to my church and my family. I attended a small Free Will Baptist church in Eau Gallie, Florida. I was loved by the church family and was molded by their instruction and belief. The thought never occurred to me that there was any other way to go about the running a church than the way they were doing it. No one questioned the method or the results. Looking back, however, that church is about the same size as it was when I attended in the early sixties. The difference is that there are only a few of the original people there. If I walked through the door next Sunday, I would be considered a visitor, a stranger. It would seem strange wearing a visitor's tag in a church that my parents helped start in someone's home in the early sixties.

As I look back, the first indication that something was wrong occurred while I was in college. I still remember the details clearly. I had moved to Nashville, Tennessee right after high school to attend college at my denomination's school. At the time, I was in my third year of college. I had been married for two years and considered myself to be a fairly mature adult. I had always been involved in some kind of singing group since junior high. In the early 1970s a college friend and I had put together an eight person vocal group that sang folk songs as well as the new Christian music that was beginning to play on the radio. We also performed original material. Groups of that era liked to dress alike, so one of the mothers of a member helped sew dresses for the girls while the guys bought shirts that matched the material of the girls' dresses. We were sharp, all the way down to the (hold your reaction please) red, white, and blue wing tip shoes! The guys, however, wore only loud red, white, and blue polyester shirts. We did not wear ties or sport coats.

We took advantage of an opportunity to sing one Sunday evening at a local church. Everything seemed to be going really well. We did notice, however, that the Dean of the college and several professors were in attendance. The next day I received a memo from the Dean to visit him in the administration office.

I walked into his office and was asked to take a seat. I still remember the smell, the polished wood shelves, the straight back chair that demanded that I sit upright, and the authoritative stare coming across the desk through the glasses of the Dean. He quickly let me know that I and the other men in the group who were enrolled at his college had violated dress protocol by not wearing a tie and coat to church. I was told that if it happened again we would be suspended. The only words that I spoke during the entire meeting were, "You will never have to worry about that again." I left.

The end result was that I transferred to another school and finished my college degree. At the time, I just considered the incident to be a consequence of attending a strict, narrow-minded school. Instead of making any trouble, I just left. Looking back, I realize that denomination has never grown and is in fact, like the denomination that I currently belong to, declining. Was that incident when I started to be concerned about the lights going out in the Little Brown Church in the Vale? On the surface no, but subconsciously, yes.

During college, I was probably about as religiously mixed up as one could get. I was technically a member of the Free Will Baptist Church; I was attending a Southern Baptist college whose theology was 180 degrees from the church to which I belonged; I married a Lutheran, and I was a part-time minister of music in a Cumberland Presbyterian church. Really, I wasn't a member of anything. In the middle of this maze of religious tension, I encountered two more events that would add to my discomfort about the "church." The first was more of a reoccurring thought. While I was dating my wife, I would occasionally pick up her brother from some class he was attending in the Lutheran faith with a name I had never heard before. He was preparing for a thing called Confirmation. My future wife had already been through this, and by high school she knew more about Christianity and her Lutheran heritage than I would learn about mine after several years of college. I often wondered why my church didn't do the same thing. It just made too much sense, and, as I would come to understand later, there were actually *expectations* of those who chose to follow this faith.

The second thing that happened during this time was that I had a confrontation with the pastor of the Cumberland Presbyterian Church where I was directing music in the early seventies. It was about music of all things. I had decided to use a classical guitar in one of the services, which I thought was a perfectly appropriate accompaniment to my song. I was called into the pastor's office later and informed that a guitar was not acceptable in his church. Well, at least I was wearing a coat and tie. I did not leave, but things were very tense for months until I left to take a full-time position in a Southern Baptist Church after graduating from college.

As it turned out, all of these experiences and more were mileposts in a journey that I wasn't even aware I was taking. The big event, the one that brought me to my knees, was yet to come. It was an event that has been repeated in church after church across America for the past several years. Again, it had to do with music, but as I would come to understand, music was not really the problem. It was merely a convenient hook on which to hang the real problem—total, unadulterated resistance to change.

I have already covered some of the details about this series of events, and I will not repeat them here. What is important is that during the next five years after I resigned, I would have time to reflect on my life and to sit back and observe the church. Also important is that during this time, for the first time, I had completely turned this over to God. What I witnessed during those five years was amazing. It was during this time that God laid on my heart the concepts that, with the help of a few of my brothers and sisters in Christ became *Our Journey*.

Having given you this additional background, I ask you to stop and think about your life in the church. It may have been a short time, or, like me, maybe you have been involved for decades. Wherever you are in your journey, it is important for you to be honest about your feelings and your conclusions. It is important that you share them with others within your circle. It only takes one individual to completely change circumstances. That one person might be you. Remember that God doesn't think like we do. He doesn't choose His leaders based on our criteria or our resume. You can make all of the excuses you want to, but if He is knocking on your door you have two choices—ignore it or answer it.

My prayer is that you will humbly walk to the door and open it. My prayer is not that you invite him in. My prayer is that you will have your hat in your hand and that you will join Jesus as you both head off on a journey that will forever change history. Yes, with God, you can do that. See you on the road. All that is left to do is finish.

Notes

1. Word Made Flesh. Serving Jesus Among the Poorest of the Poor. 2008. June 23, 2008. http://www.wordmadeflesh.org/
2. The Little Brown Church In the Vale. Little Brown Church History. 2008. June 23, 2008. http://www.littlebrownchurch.org/churchhistory.cfm
3. The Barna Group. The Barna Update. Unchurched Population Nears 100 Million in the US. March 19, 2007. http://www.barna.org/FlexPage.aspx?Page=BarnaUpdateNarrowPreview&BarnaUpdateID=267
4. American Society for Church Growth (ASCG.) Enlarging Our Boarders. Report presented to the Executive Presbytery. January, 1999.
5. Earley, Dave. July 17, 2006. Liberty University. The Desperate Need For New Churches. https://www.liberty.edu/media/1162/cmt/The%20Desperate%20Need%20for%20New%20Churches%202%20page.doc
6. PlusLine. Sponsored by the North American Division of Seventh-day Adventists and your local Union Conference.
7. Barnes, Rebecca and Linda Lowry. May 1, 2006. North American Mission Board. Special Report: The American Church in Crisis. http://www.namb.net/site/apps/nl/content3.asp?c=9qKILUOzEpH&b=1594355&ct=2350673

8. Olson, David T. 2004. The American Church Research Project. Theamericanchurch.org. Twelve Surprising Facts About the American Church. http://www.theamericanchurch.org/sample/12SurprisingFactsSample.ppt
9. Stanley, Andy, Reggie Joiner, Lane Jones, *7 Practices of Effective Ministry*, Multnomah Publishers, Inc, 2004
10. Dunkelberg, Pete. Irreducible Complexity Demystified, http://www.talkdesign.org/faqs/icdmyst/ICDmyst.html.argument
11. Guin, Jay. December 18, 2007. One In Jesus. Oneinjesus.info. Church Growth:National Trends. http://oneinjesus.info/2007/12/18/church-growth-national-trends/
12. McIntosh, Gary L., *One Church, Four Generations,* published by Baker Books, 2004.
13. Harvey, H. Thomas, professor of ecology, San Jose University, *the Sequoias of Yosemite National Park,* published by the Yosemite Association in cooperation with the National Park service, 1978, 4th reprint 1991
14. Erwin, Gayle, *The Jesus Style*, Word Publishing, 1988

About the Author

Bob G. Shupe

Mr. Shupe is a past Moderator of the Nashville Presbytery of the Cumberland Presbyterian Church. He has served on their Cross-Cultural Task Force for the past eight years working with Sudanese Christians who desire to establish a church in America. He was one of the original members of *Malachi*, a Christian Rock Band for twenty years, including two music mission trips to Colombia, South America. Mr. Shupe has served as the music coordinator for the Cumberland Presbyterian Board of Missions for two Missions conferences and has served the Tusculum Church, at different times, as Minister of Music since 1968. Mr. Shupe's lay ministry, *Brother Bob Ministries*, has lectured across the south east on many different subjects related to church growth. He teaches various educational classes in his church and is an active elder. He is a graduate of Belmont University, with a degree in Church Music.

On the secular side Mr. Shupe owns and operates an insurance consulting firm with his wife and son, consulting on several public entities in Tennessee. He is the author of several industry articles and a book on the high cost of healthcare, *the Bitter Pill, where did my benefits go?* He is active in state and federal politics working as the state legislative director of the National Association of Health Underwriters.

Mr. Shupe is currently working on a soon to be released novel about the devastating effect of national health care on the U.S. economy, should it be passed. He is the father of two grown children, a grandfather and the husband of Valerie Shupe for the past thirty-nine years.

Contact Information

If you would like more information or if you would be interested in having Mr. Shupe hold a seminar, retreat or speak to your group, please contact him at bob@esptn.com.

If you would like to order additional books of ten or more at a discounted price please email at sue@tuculumchurch.org. Please order single books up to nine through your book store or online at Wheatmark.com, Amazon or Barnes and Noble.

For a closer look at *Our Journey*, developed by the Tusculum Church, please visit, www.tusculumchurch.org and click on the *Our Journey* tab on the menu.

Printed in the United States
123855LV00004B/319-336/P